BUBBLEHEADS

THE MED RUN

STEVEN BROCK

Book Cover Design by Savannah Brock

ISBN-13: 978-0-692-16617-8

Second Edition

Although the USS Lapon was a real submarine, this book is fictional. Any resemblance to a person or persons either living or dead is purely coincidental.

Even though you may think it's you, it's not.

Trust me.

FOREWORD

There are so many, many books you can read, fiction and non-fiction, about submarining from both famous and not so famous authors. In 'Bubbleheads', first time author Steven Brock attempts and in my opinion succeeds, in bringing to life on these pages the true stories of what it is like to serve on board one of our nation's nuclear submarines.

Taking place during the Cold War with the Soviet Union, Steve takes you on a journey from raising your right hand and swearing in to serve our nation, to life in Boot Camp in Orlando, Florida and Nuclear Power School, and then with orders in hand (and Butterflies in the stomach) to a submarine in Norfolk, Virginia. And then finally the incredible journey to getting underway and heading out on deployment.

Steve also shares with great candor the trials and tribulations of long separations, and sometimes the heart break caused by the lack of contact with family members for weeks at a time. He relates with honesty and true feeling to the reader what it is like to be underway, and also what the families of these men, and now women, go through back home while these submarines are on deployment for so long on the front lines of service to our nation.

To those of you who have served on submarines, I promise that you will relate to so many of these stories contained on these pages. I am sure many of them will bring back your own memories, sea stories, faces from your past and a smile to your face as you reconnect and remember your own individual journeys. With incredible wit and humor, facts, and a knack for sharing even the smallest moments and details of the journey, the reader will feel almost like he or she is along on this adventure to and from the Mediterranean Sea.

For those who have never served onboard or have never even set foot on a submarine, this book will take you along for an incredible ride. Feel free to let yourself go and immerse yourself in this fascinating tale of life as a young submariner on an incredible trip. For some of you, it will make your jealous that you did not have the opportunity. For some of you younger folks, maybe this will be the incentive you need to go see a recruiter! ☺

Thanks for a great ride down memory lane for me Steve, and the opportunity to share my thoughts with your readers ... all my best to you and your family ….. and THANK YOU for your service to our country. Bravo Zulu !

Keith

Keith F. Post, Executive Director
St. Marys Submarine Museum
St. Marys, Georgia

ACKNOWLEDGEMENTS

The actual putting words to paper was singular. However, there was a world of support of family and friends that helped me through the process.

First, my family. My wife, Patty, has endured it all. My frustrations, doubts, procrastinations, and leaving the toilet seat up. She offered words of encouragement when she read the manuscript. Told me I could do it. She believed in me. If there was a dedication, I would dedicate it to her.

My son, Justin, and daughter, Savannah, were also encouraging. I don't recall a single time they rolled their eyes when I proclaimed my New Year's Resolution was finishing the book…again. In addition, Savannah did a great job designing the front and back covers.

Ritchie Watson was a tremendous help by giving me a pdf of the errors which were mostly incorporated in this 2nd edition.

Special thanks to Keith, Gianna and the staff at St Marys Submarine Museum near Kings Bay, Ga. They have sponsored two book signings thus far and also invited me to listen to Vice Admiral Konetzni's presentation on the future of submarines. I highly recommend a visit to this historic submarine museum. You won't be disappointed.

My childhood friend, Eddie Rodgers got me my first book signing at the Aiken County Historical Museum. You can catch him portraying General Wade Hampton during the Battle of Aiken reenactment.

Thanks to the real men I served with on the USS Lapon. I couldn't ask for a finer bunch of men to punch holes in the ocean.

Sunday, 02/08/81

Duncan Keller had just finished securing the galley. Made of gleaming stainless steel, it was so bright it almost made him squint. As he gave himself a satisfactory nod, he noticed a small smudge on the mixer. Since the outside of his t-shirt was a tad bit smudgy itself, he pulled out his t-shirt and used the inside of it to remove the smudge. After surveying the rest of the galley, he nodded once again with satisfaction.

The mess decks were filled with sailors, bellies full of canned roast beef, instant potatoes and rehydrated peas. Many considered Duncan a magician for his ability to take military canned meat and dehydrated vegetables (which has a shelf life that rivals the half-life of uranium) and convert it into something that actually tasted good.

"Duncan," Petty Officer Carter would often say as he rubbed his enormous belly. "You are going to make some woman a good wife."

A low hum of conversation was floating up from four guys at the table in the back when suddenly laughter bubbled up from the middle. At that precise moment the sub, their home for the last twenty-three days lurched suddenly upward, then jerked to the port side. From underneath the boat came a long shriek as the sub

1

groaned and shuddered. A sickening crunch from the bow of the boat was followed by muffled popping noises, and then silence.

For a frozen second, panic flashed across Duncan's face as he held onto the counter he had just painstakingly polished. The collision alarm caused an eruption of arms and legs as hours upon hours of training superseded fear and panic. An unfamiliar voice bellowed from the 1 Main Circuit (1MC) speaker in the overhead:

"FLOODING IN THE TORPEDO ROOM!

FLOODING IN THE TORPEDO ROOM!"

A phone-talker stationed himself quickly in the aft portion of the mess decks, just above the ladder leading down to the torpedo room. Petty Officer (PO) Carter, the first on the scene in the torpedo room, was barking out status reports from just inside the fake wood-paneled door as icy cold seawater circled around his ankles.

Again, the 1MC crackled to life: "REACTOR SCRAM! REACTOR SCRAM! RIG SHIP FOR REDUCED ELECTRICAL!" Carter looked up at the loudspeaker and winced. 'We just lost propulsion.' He glanced over at the phone-talker, Seaman Timmy Garland on his first deployment aboard the USS Millard Fillmore, one of the Navy's oldest fast attack submarines. His mouth was slack-jawed and his eyes looked like a frightened caged animal.

"Don't worry son." PO Carter assured him. "She's a tough old boat and we've got the best crew in the Navy. We'll pull out of this one."

The sub was listing heavily to the starboard side and slowly its nose started to sink. Over the 1MC, the Officer of the Deck, Lieutenant Oscar Underhill, commanded "EMERGENCY BLOW!"

A whoosh of compressed air pushed the intruding seawater from the ballast tanks. The nose of the sub angled upward, and slowly started to rise. A cheer went up on the mess decks and PO Carter muttered under his breath, 'Come on, Girl. You can do it!"

Back slaps and high fives were plentiful now. Smiles and shouts broke out: "Splice the Main Brace!", "AMEN","Is there any pie left?", "Nah, the Ward Room got it."

Then, as they became aware that the boat's ascent had stopped and started to slip downward, laughter died and dread overtook the crew once again.

Meanwhile, underneath in the Torpedo Room, four men, battling the seawater spewing from a busted flange, were waist-deep in the incoming seawater, chilled and soaked to the bone. PO Carter bit his lip, closed his eyes and thought of his wife and daughter. Two levels up, in the Control Room, the Officer of the Deck (OOD), standing behind the Diving Officer, softly asked, "What's our depth?"

The Diving Officer, Master Chief Levar Hunter, answered just as quietly, "Six hundred and thirty feet, sir…and falling."

The OOD turned around, mumbled something, and keyed the 1MC, "Sonar, Con. What's our sounding?"

A small voice answered, "Con, Sonar. Four thousand seven hundred and fifty feet."

"Sonar, Con. Aye." The OOD assessed the situation: no propulsion, the flooding hasn't stopped and we are dropping like a rock." He glanced over at the Diving Officer. Master Chief Levar Hunter, almost imperceptibly, shook his head.

The depth gauge passed a thousand feet, and still the crippled boat sank. The OOD announced that they were heading beyond crush depth. There was nothing left to do but wait. He kept staring at the depth gauge as it ran by fifteen hundred feet. From back aft came a horrendous roar. He closed his eyes and thought, 'I hope it's painless.'

At this moment, I woke up wide-eyed, sweating and gasping for air, as though I had just run five miles. Scanning the room quickly confirmed that I was still in a motel just outside of Norfolk, Virginia. A dream. I blinked twice. It was just a dream.

My name is Garrett Daniels, the self-appointed Scribe of these Sea Scrolls. Not a diary, mind you, a journal. Girls keep diaries; men keep journals. Hemmingway kept journals. At least, I think he did. Well, I know he didn't keep a diary. Or if he did, he would have called it a journal. ANYWAY, I have not always been a submariner. In fact, this will be my first time aboard a submarine.

I was born and raised in Aiken, South Carolina. There are two things Aiken is known for: horse racing and it's near the Masters Golf Tournament in Augusta, Georgia.

In Aiken, I often spent summer days looking for a creek to swim in. Cold Creek was often the choice, but if we had a little money, we'd head off to Richardson's Lake. Winters were mild, we rarely got snow…but wait, this journal is not about Aiken or my childhood days. This journal is to log in my experiences in the Navy, specifically on a sub.

I woke up from that dream at 4:32AM in a motel just outside of Norfolk. Guess I shouldn't have had that last piece of sausage pizza the night before. The dream was more than a little unnerving. In just a few hours, I would be reporting aboard the USS Lapon, hull number SSN 661. I knew absolutely nothing about this boat except that it was tied up to Pier 23 at the Norfolk Naval Command Base, D&S Piers. In just a few hours that boat will be my home for the next four years.

Tuesday, 03/03/81

I had been assigned to the USS Lapon, a Sturgeon class fast-attack nuclear sub in Submarine Command Force 6. Sturgeon-class submarines are named after different freshwater and saltwater fish. Apparently a Lapon is a fish of some sort. I don't know where they swim but I know we don't have them back home.

There are two types of subs currently in the US Navy: fast-attacks and boomers. The basic differences are the size and speed. Boomers are almost twice as large because they house missiles in their midsection. But fast attacks are...well faster.

Over the last month the Lapon had been preparing for a deployment. The surface rust on the sail and the fair-weather planes have been wire-brushed and touched up with green primer paint and a new layer of flat black paint. Below decks, every piece of equipment was checked for operation and stowed for sea duty.

Today was "Stores Load" day. After lunch, each division had to send a "volunteer" to help load all the food needed to feed a crew of 126 men for the next month. Guess who the

"E" Division (E-Div) volunteer was? Yep. Since I was the most junior member on board, that happened a lot.

For Stores Load, a long line of sailors formed from the pier, down the brow, through the Weapons Loading Hatch, along the upper passageway, down a stairwell to the Galley on the second deck. A human conveyor belt. I was positioned under the Weapons Loaded Hatch, reaching up for a box, then shifting and turning to pass it to the next guy.

When the day was over I grabbed a quick bite, and headed over to the Basic Enlisted Quarters (BEQ), which is where submariners are housed when they are in port. This is not the Ritz. The rooms are very basic: bunk beds which can be broken down to make two twin beds, two identical closets, two identical night stands, two identi …Well you get the idea. Since there is no TV, I flopped down on my rack, a little sore from lifting the seemingly endless boxes of cans and frozen goods, and closed my eyes.

As I look back, it seems that it took forever to get here. Even though it was only two years ago when I first walked into a Navy Enlistment Office to talk to a recruiter, Chief Petty Officer (CPO) Richard F. Palmeroy. When I walked into the Navy Recruiting Office, squeezed between an Eckerd and a sub sandwich joint (ironic, isn't it?), he was standing in front of a large framed picture of an aircraft carrier. A deep blue ceramic cup with a gold anchor, filled with black steaming coffee was secured in his right hand. The pressed white collar on his shirt was wrapped too tightly around his neck, giving the appearance his shirt was squeezing his head and neck out.

He rotated that head, topped with a short blondish crew cut, looked over at me, then checked his watch. "Good, Mr. Daniels. Right on time. The Navy loves men who are prompt." His head snapped back to face the picture once again.

"You see that?" He flicked his wrist forward and a finger shot out. "That's an Aircraft Carrier. The U.S.S. Enterprise. The most feared ship in the world, but do you know what an aircraft carrier fears the most?"

"No...uh...sir."

"Don't call me sir son. I'm not an officer. I work for a living." He paused briefly, then slowly turned, "An aircraft carrier fears a submarine."

As he turned to me, his chest came into full view. Good God, I thought. It was chock full of all sorts of medals and rows upon rows of ribbons. With the speech and the medals and uniform and the steaming black coffee and the aircraft carrier, well...I was hooked. And...he knew it.

I can only remember bits and pieces of our conversation after that. He convinced me to volunteer for submarines and the Naval Nuclear Power Program, sight unseen ("They are the elite of the Navy, he said "the astronauts of the sea."). And then added with a small tilt and a shake of his head, "Hey, now...There is absolutely no problem in getting the place of duty you want. I'm sure you've heard horror stories in the old days of a sailor requesting, let's say Charleston as a home port, and getting Guam or something like that. That's the way it used to be in the old navy. That's history. We are the "New Navy". We've computerized things quite a bit".

I can still see the him smile, straighten up and raise his eyebrows as he emphasized the word "New". You could tell he had some experience in sales but wasn't quite polished yet. I had no clue back then but I have since narrowed it down to used cars or Amway. But, at the time, it didn't stop me from lapping it up. For CPO Palmeroy, recruiting me must have been like shooting fish in a barrel.

In no time, I was saying good bye to my friends and family, swearing in at Fort Jackson in Columbia, S.C. Then off to six weeks of boot camp in Orlando, and after that, 24 months of training in different schools in various locations all over the country. But the last year wasn't easy. First there were six months of Nuclear Power School in Orlando.

During the last month, I was on five-hours-a-night mandatory study time. The next six months covered Prototype training on an operating Nuclear Reactor. The final test was in two parts, a fill-in-the-blank-no-multiple-guess-four-hour test and then stand-up-in-front-of-six-people-while-they-pepper-you-with-questions-and-make-you-feel-like-an-idiot oral exams ("So, Petty Officer Daniels, are you really trying to tell us that nuclear fission is like *Pop Rocks* going off in your mouth?").

Upon completion of Prototype, you receive a "dream sheet" to fill out with your top three choices for home port. This is where a fully trained, but not yet qualified, nuke submariner would finally get to see his first submarine. I requested San Diego third, Norfolk second and Charleston first (since I'm from South Carolina). I got Norfolk. Which, I've heard is not a surprise. It's like flying anywhere in the southeast. Your first stop will always be Atlanta, the joke is, after you die, whether you are going to heaven or hell, you have to first stop in Atlanta. Well, Norfolk is the Navy's Atlanta.

Sleep is catching up to me now, memories fading in and out...the night at the lake, Candice (don't call her Candy!) in her halter top and jean cutoffs waving good-bye, Dorchester and the redhead, the celebrations of graduation, the agony

10

when Wesley threw away all of his training for a girl he barely knew. Even though all that happened two years ago, and at the time it seemed like the longest two years of my life, today, right now, this minute, it seems like the shortest. And, you know, in the back of my mind when I signed up for submarines in that recruiter's office, somehow, I never thought I would actually be on one.

Well, I am. And tomorrow we leave our berth at D & S Piers in the Norfolk Naval Base for a five-month Med Run which, I found out, means a Mediterranean tour of duty. Even though it says "Mediterranean" tour, we could actually go anywhere. There's a cloak of secrecy about what we do and where we are, and for good reason. We are alone in what we do. We don't get ground cover or air support. Hopefully, surface ships wouldn't even know where we are anyway. Our missions, for the most part, are singular in design. There are times when we travel with a surface fleet in transit overseas. But our mission is to protect them, not vice versa. Besides, the Navy won't confirm or deny our position. Kind of like the disclaimer on the Mission Impossible tape before it self-destructs. We'll spend time patrolling, running different ops, and occasionally visit a few ports (which I am really looking forward to). Even though I have never been overseas, I have been to more places and done more things in the past two years than in my entire twenty-two years on this earth. Navy Schools have taken me from Orlando to the Great Lakes, back to Orlando and then to New York. So, after investing all of that money in training me, it was time for the Navy to assign me to my first submarine.

Wednesday 03/04/81

I didn't sleep well last night. Today we leave home port and won't come back for five months. I drove off base and headed down Hampton Boulevard to get a sausage biscuit and coffee. Hard to believe I wouldn't see any of this for quite some time.

The place was near empty when I pulled in to the parking lot. Two newspaper stands stood guard side by side at the entrance. After scanning the headlines, I fumbled for change, dropped a quarter in the slot and bought my last newspaper for the next five months.

"Reagan: Larger Navy needed to Match Soviets", "Prince Charles to attend NY Ballet" "Hunger Strike in Ireland Continues" screamed the headlines. And more locally "Auto Repair Shop Owner Death Suspicious", "Arson Suspected at Nursing Home" and "It's Ash Wednesday". Okay maybe some of this stuff I won't miss, but at least there are the comics. With breakfast and newspaper in hand, I headed back to D&S Piers, although a part of me wanted to turn around and go somewhere, anywhere else.

13

I parked my Nova in the D&S Piers parking lot, (I have trouble remembering where I parked at the mall. How would I remember where I parked after 5 months?), and locked her up for the last time. It's so hard to fathom that. You go away for a vacation and come back after a week and things seem familiar but out of sorts. How familiar will things be in August? One thing for sure the temperature will be different.

The wind was cold and salty as I made my way down to the sub. In the distance, the Executive Officer, (XO) second in command, was just returning from his morning run. I wish I had his energy. A health nut and an exercise fanatic, he wears gym shorts more than a uniform while in port.

The sub was getting closer. Maybe something would happen that would keep me from getting on that sub. I could be shot or kidnapped, or trip and break a leg, or have a stroke.

No such luck. "Down the hatch, past the guns, look out Med, here I come".

Friday 03/06/81

I had envisioned writing in this journal every day. I have since found out that this is impossible. Two days have gone by since we pulled out of port and headed out to sea. I also found out that when the sub leaves the pier, it doesn't dive immediately. First off, the topside crew is still, well, topside. They are securing the tie lines, stowing away other stuff and waving goodbye to everyone on the pier and along the shore. John Graham, my roommate at the BEQ when the sub is pier side, is an "A-ganger" and one of the topside crew. (A-ganger means he is a non-nuclear machinist mate).

It was purely a stroke of luck that I was assigned to room with him. We hit it off from day one because we both like country music. When I first walked in to the barracks after reporting for duty, I could hear Hank Jr. blaring down the hallway. When I got to the room, I found out exactly where the music was coming from. I could see this guy in front of a mirror getting ready to go out. I yelled out over the music that Bocephus sent me. John spun around from the mirror, saw my hat, and then gave me a big grin.

"You like Hank?" he asked.

"Yeah," I answered back with my own grin. "It's a family tradition. Garrettt Daniels", I extended my hand.

"John Graham," he replied returning the handshake, "but everyone calls me Cracker."

Well, that was that. We had about three weeks left in port before the Med Run, my first time at sea. Besides filling me in on the best country bars in town (the Fifth National Bank was a favorite stop), he'd been preparing me for life at sea. For nukes, if you are not on watch, there is not a lot to do while steaming out of port. The forward pukes, are more involved, including the Topside and Bridge Crew. They are the last people to experience the outside world before being sealed up below decks. There are other advantages besides being the last to breathe fresh air and feel the sun on their faces. But those are not the best reasons for being topside.

As the sub made its way down the Chesapeake River, topless girls would race by in their boats and wave to the guys topside as they head out to sea. They do that not only to the subs, but also to what submariners call surface ships.

Of course, that made me wish I could be assigned to the Topside Crew. But they won't let the nukes do it. Too expensive to replace or not coordinated enough to handle the ropes? Too close to call. Subs don't have guardrails. There is, however, a track just slightly to the portside, that runs along the deck from bow to stern. All of the topside crew wear a harness attached to the track with a metal clip which slides along the track. After the topside crew stows everything, they head down below. The only people left are those on the bridge which, while we are on the surface, is located at the very top of the sail. There's an OOD in charge, a lookout and a phone-talker. The OOD in this case is our Captain, James T. Kirk. Just kidding. Captain Jack Hammer had been the skipper on the USS Lapon for the past two years, with just one year left on his rotation of sea duty. From what I hear, he is "Old School" Navy and extremely bright. John told me that since Captain Jack's been on board, the crew's morale has done a 180 turnaround. When in port, be it at home port or some remote port of call, the Captain instructs the XO that the crew, as much as humanly possible, should be on liberty. He instructs the Yeoman to set up tours, trips and meals at restaurants at reduced rates through his many contacts in Norfolk, the Med and other places where the sub pulls in. The locals at whichever port they happen to be in will gather on the pier to greet him. It's not surprising to see Captain Jack light up some cigars and drink beer with some of the most common folk you can imagine and he looks like he is genuinely enjoying himself.

It's the OOD's job to guide the boat safely out through the harbor to the open ocean. The ride through the harbor is peaceful and steady. If you are below deck, you can barely tell that you are not tied up to the pier. You feel no sense of motion. However, once you get to open water, that can quickly change. It never occurred to me that it would be a rough ride on the surface. That wasn't the picture my recruiter had painted. When a sub gets out to the open sea, it seems more like a cork than a boat because it has no keel. It simply rides on top of the waves. As if you went into the ocean and floated on your back. You could feel every rise and fall of the waves.

I didn't think to bring seasick pills, but I did have a lot of Rolaids which I popped like candy. Still, I must confess, I was getting a little queasy. Since it was my first time at sea and I wasn't qualified to do anything, I headed down to the mess decks. Boy, that was a mistake. Food was really not what I needed to smell. There were some "old salts" on the mess decks who like to have some fun with those who were a little green under the gills. Chief Garrison and Chief Ramirez, (the Chief of the Boat, COB), John and a few other enlisted men would order special concoctions from Tony the Mess Cook which are designed to make the new guys (who are called Dink, non-qual, OBNL which stands for Oxygen Breathing

No Load) puke. The COB is the highest-ranking enlisted person on board. While other officers will come and go, the COB stays with his boat; therefore, he knows more about that boat and its capabilities than anyone else. Nobody calls him Chief Ramirez anymore; they just call him COB.

When John yelled at me to come over and join them, I took a vacant spot next to Chief Garrison, desperately trying to hide the fact that my stomach was rolling.

"Here," John said with an amused smile. "Try this special recipe that Tony cooked up. His grandmother brought it over from Italy."

He handed me a bowl with a mixture that looked like creamed corn with mustard, hot sauce and, I think, boiled eggs. Tony Vinelli, a New Yorker was tall, and thin, with thick black hair and a huge black mustache perched over his dazzling white teeth. And, boy, could he cook. The spices and flavoring he uses in his cooking takes a normal Navy meal to a whole new level.

By now the aroma of his mixture was getting strong and my stomach started to churn. "If Tony's grandmother brought that over from Italy, I bet the rest of the crew didn't make it," I said weakly.

"Let me try a bite of your grandma's recipe," Chief Melvin E. Garrison, our division E-Division Lead. He was slightly overweight and his khaki shirt was at least one size too small. His black and white peppered hair was closely cropped on the top of his head and his matching chest hair sprouted out over the top of his t-shirt as if it was trying to escape. The furry carpet of hair curled over his sleeves as it traveled down his arms and almost completely covered up the various Navy slogans tattooed on both forearms. Someone had told me that he even had the word "NAVY" tattooed on his butt. While there is no doubt that the tattoo exists, I wondered if it, too, was lost in all that hair. He was commonly called a "lifer-dog".

Chief Garrison took a spoon, scooped some of Tony's grandma's "recipe" into his mouth and, instead of swallowing it, he turned to me and smiled with an open mouth. Well, that did it. Everything that had been in my stomach for the past six hours made a surprise appearance all over the mess deck. There was a split second of silence, then several people shouted "yes" and high fives were passed around. John was laughing as he slapped my back, "Welcome aboard non-qual!" About that time, some of us noticed that the COB was looking down at the floor, or so we thought. John leaned over from his seat to see what the COB was looking at. I already knew and opened my mouth to speak, but no words came out. My mouth was moving but the only noise I could make was a "cuh, cuh, cuh". John burst out laughing again and shouted, "Look! He got some CORN ON THE COB!" Sure enough, when I heaved, it hit the deck with such velocity that it splashed onto COB's shoe. Then the COB slowly lifted his head, turned to look at me and said with a slight smile that had no real humor behind it, "OK, dink, now clean this crap up."

Since that day, the USS Lapon has slipped underneath the ocean's surface and now life under the sea was almost like being tied up to a pier.

My stomach has since returned to normal because, once under the waves, there is no sense of motion and, contrary to popular belief, there are no viewing windows like 20,000 Leagues under the Sea which may have been some people's inspiration to volunteer for submarine duty.

Volunteering for subs is the only way to get on one, or at least it's the first step. The forward pukes (those who did not go to nuke school), have to attend Sub School in Groton. I hear that one of the things you have to do, is get in the bottom of a giant tower of water with a Steinke Hood on, then they flood it and you float to the top. A Steinke Hood is a life preserver with a hood. The hood and life preserver are filled with air and used when leaving through the escape hatch if a sub becomes disabled in relatively shallow water.

Sub School also weeds out people who might freak out when they finally get inside a real sub and close all the hatches. Except for the long transit on surface before we dive, the sub is very stable. It's like living in a three-story tube with more stuff crammed inside than it was designed to hold. Cables and pipes snake in and out in the overhead, dodging light fixtures and equipment.

On the morning, we left while flipping through the radio channels one last time, I heard a song "Don't Stand So Close to Me". Now underway, as we turn sideways to pass each other in the passageways, I can hear that chorus playing in my head. While in port, the whole crew is not on the boat at the same time. Now the place is crawling with people.

Because of the transit across the Atlantic Ocean, there is more canned food on board than storage compartments can hold. Piles of cans of all sizes, full of every kind of vegetable filled the passageway floor from the mess decks all the way back to the berthing compartment. That makes the passageway seem even shorter than it is. I've seen Tony walking on those cans down that passageway, bent way over to avoid hitting the stuff in the overhead.

The mess decks are located about amidships of the sub on the second level, and the main berthing compartment is all the way forward of the mess decks in the front or bow of the

22

sub. In fact, it's called the Bow Compartment and houses most of the crew, including the chiefs who have a separate berthing compartment off to the left (port) side of the Bow Compartment, commonly known as the "Goat Locker". It reminds me of the inside of a Winnebago because it's longer than it is wide, and everything is compacted into a small space. The layout of the Goat Locker begins with the sleeping quarters in the forward part, with racks on either side of a narrow walkway. Just aft of their sleeping quarters is a small table with a large coffee pot and benches that will seat four depending on the size of the Chiefs who sit there. Aft of the table is the "head," or bathroom, containing a stainless-steel shower, sink and commode.

There are other smaller berthing compartments, named for the number of people who can fit in it, like the 6-Man or 18-man. Just aft of the Bow compartment are the crew's showers and toilets, referred to as the "head". Everything structural is made of stainless steel. The commodes are especially unusual, because to flush them, you first have to turn a valve to "cut in" some seawater. After the desired amount of flushing water is added, then you rotate forward a huge 3-foot plastic-covered handle that sticks up on the left side of the commode. This operates a ball valve in the bottom of the commode which does the flushing. There must be some vacuum on the other side, because it looks like it is actually sucked in.

The COB had issued me a rack (bed) in the Bow Compartment before we left port. I was familiar with them from standing 24-hour duty in port. When, E-Div is in port, our normal duty section, called "three section duty", is once every three days. When on duty, you are confined to the boat for 24 hours, from 0800 to 0800. Weekends, weekdays, holidays, it doesn't matter. If duty falls on a Monday, then Tuesday morning at 0800 that duty section is relieved from duty. However, they may still have to stay on the boat for training, meetings or regular work. Normally, a chance to sleep will fall somewhere during the night of your duty section and racks are assigned for that purpose. However; while in port, submariners stay in assigned Basic Enlisted Quarters (BEQ) on base for free. Some submariners choose to rent a house or apartment somewhere off base out of their own pockets. Often, two, three or more will rent together to split the cost.

Now these racks on the sub remind me of beds on a train. Picture them after squeezing the beds of four sleeping cars into the space of one. The walkway in between the racks is barely shoulder width. The rack looks like a steel coffin with one side removed. A blue cloth curtain runs the length of the opening for some measure of privacy. At the head of the bed, there's an 8-watt fluorescent light fixture mounted right above the pillow. So, while you are stretched out in the rack, that light fixture is six inches or less from your head. Good for reading, but a word of advice here: turn your head first either to the right or left before you sneeze or you will wind up with little grate marks from the light fixture on your forehead.

In this particular location, three additional racks are stacked on top of mine. I got the bottom rack, not unusual for a first-timer. The really choice racks are the top ones. The reasoning is simple. If the rack is on the bottom, it's at foot level with all of its aromas. If the rack is in the middle, that's your basic butt level. To me, this is the least desirable rack level. Since no women are, have been or can be assigned to a sub, men are free to say and do whatever they want. Strong language is heard occasionally, except around Captain Jack, who does not tolerate it and will have you written up under the laws of the Uniform Code of Military Justice (UCMJ). But farting is fair game and pretty common-place. There's been talk about women who actually want to serve on a submarine. They have no clue what they are asking for, unless they, too, participate in that sort of behavior. But would you really want to hear a woman burp? Or fart?

There are activities that woman do that you would just rather not know about.

But the biggest reason the Navy has not allowed women on subs yet is not discrimination or fear of pregnancy, or even the strong language. Some women can hold their own in that department. No, the biggest reason not to have women aboard a sub is so men can fart freely whenever and wherever they want to, without having to apologize. We hate apologizing for farting because, we are proud of our farts. In fact, the loudest, longest or smelliest farts are applauded and revered. That's a freedom that would be difficult to give up.

It's easy to see why the top rack, above most of the body odors, makes it more desirable. The disadvantage to a top rack is getting into them. There are no ladders, so you have to find pipes or something in the overhead in order to pull yourself up by your hands, then swing your feet up into the rack and scoot in.

Underneath the thin mattress is a storage compartment that runs the length of the rack, deep enough to store clothes and other non-valuable things. For valuables, there is a lockable storage box about the size a glove compartment, mounted on the ceiling at the foot of the rack. Along with my rack, the COB issued me three sets of "poopie suits". Don't let the name fool you. You don't poopie in them. They are actually one-piece, long-sleeved, all-cotton jump suits we wear while we are underway. Before we left, John told me to buy a comfortable pair of tennis shoes. It's one of the few benefits we get while at sea that the surface ships don't. Instead of work blues and steel-toed ankle boots, called chukka boots, we wear "poopie suits" and tennis shoes. After four days of walking on steel decking (no carpeting here or vacuum cleaners...which figures because we are guys and we hate the noise of vacuum cleaners. Seriously like nails on a chalkboard.), my feet definitely prefer the tennis shoes over those steel-toed boots.

I'm sitting on the mess decks now. There are five tables with bench seats which accommodate all 113 sailors, but not at the same time. The officers have their own dining area, called the "Wardroom", which is across the hall from the crew's mess. There is a small mini-kitchen called the Wardroom Pantry right behind the Wardroom. Just aft of that is the crew's galley, complete with its own Cook. Squeezed in between the Wardroom Pantry and the Galley is the coffee mess, a milk dispenser, ice bin and the 'Bug Juice' machine. Bug juice is like Kool-Aid, but a lot more acidic. Stories float around about what a good cleanser bug juice is. Tony uses it to scrub down the grill. John uses it to clean deck plating, and I've even heard that it's used to polish the Wardroom's brass.

Just aft of the door to the galley is a pass-thru window where the mess cooks pass food to the "Cranks". This is another tradition that nukes are not normally a part of. A crank is a waiter, janitor, dishwasher and overall go-fer. The mess cooks cook. The cranks do everything else. Definitely not a job I would like. However, if you get on a crank's good side he will reward you with faster service. No tipping is allowed, but an easy signature (sig) on a man's qualification (Qual) card is appreciated.

The bench seats in the mess decks are hollow for storage, and the walls are covered with white melamine panels, some of which can also be removed for storage. A TV sits on the forward starboard side of the mess decks, next to the corpsman's office door. Doc Baker is our Corpsman on board, the only official medical personnel aboard a fast-attack submarine while at sea.

After the 1800 meal, unless there is training scheduled, it's movie time on the mess decks. Someone is designated to operate the movie projector which is set up in front of Doc's office. His usual seat is just to the right of the projector, along with a coffee and a Louis Lamour book. A screen is set up in the aft section. Before we left, I helped load in 60 or 70 movies reels, individually packaged in an olive-green case with cloth straps. I saw a few titles I recognized, like "Star Wars", "10" and "Every Which way but Loose.". There are no brand-new releases.

Two stairwells, one going up and one down, are located in the aft section. Just aft of the stairwells are a freezer, storage space, and Trash Disposal Unit (TDU). The up stairwell leads to the upper or first level of the boat and to the Engineering Spaces in the aft half, the Weapons Loading Hatch and the Control Room. The down stairwell leads to the laundry room, Machinery One and Torpedo Room.

The Trash Disposal Unit is an oversized trash compacter. How the boat gets rid of its trash is pretty impressive. First, a perforated three-foot high sheet of metal is manually rolled into a cylinder and a separate circular sheet of metal is attached to one end of the cylinder to form the bottom. Next, the finished assembly is placed under what appears to be a vertical battering ram, add circular weight at the bottom of the cylinder, and the day's trash is ready to be compacted. When the cylinder is full, the steel battering ram, pushed by 3000 pounds of hydraulics, compacts the trash and then retracts to allow more trash to be piled in. This continues until the cylinder can hold no more trash. Then, another weight is added on top, and the cylinder is sealed. After a few full cylinders have accumulated, permission is obtained by the Chief of the Watch (COW) in the Control Room to eject the cylinders through the bottom of the boat to its final resting place at the bottom of the sea. This is accomplished by a vertical torpedo tube looking device located in the aft part of the cramped TDU Room. Eventually each division on the boat will be responsible for compacting its trash, and the most junior person of that division is assigned to the task.

I have just finished a meal of roast beef, fresh potatoes and green beans. I say "fresh" because, in a couple more days, we'll be out of eggs, milk, fresh vegetables…in fact, anything that is not canned or frozen has to be eaten within a week or it will spoil. Once we eat up the fresh foods, the cans will start disappearing from the passageway.

The day at sea is split into four six-hour segments, and the mess decks serve food at the end of each segment. The only way you can tell whether it's night or day is by what is being served on the mess decks. Breakfast is served at 0600, lunch at 1200, dinner at 1800 and Midrats at midnight. Midrats will usually consist of a soup made up of leftovers from the day's meals, plus sandwiches with bologna or peanut butter and jelly. Generally, I wake up, eat whatever meal they are serving and then go stand a six-hour watch. When that watch is finished at 1200, I eat lunch, then check the Plan of the Day (POD) to see if I need to attend training classes or obtain signatures on my qualification card (after qualifying, a pin called "Dolphins" is presented to the person who has completed his qualification) or there might even be a ship's casualty drill scheduled.

At 1800, I am back in the rack to sleep until midnight, then start the next cycle of three-section duty. I get up, eat midrats and go stand a six-hour watch. In that 24-hour period, I stood watches for 12 hours, studied for four and got almost six hours of sleep. Just think, I volunteered for this! It could be a lot worse though. Occasionally on a sub, a few people stand a "port & starboard" watch. That means, after they stand a six-hour watch, they sleep, shave, do training or drills for five hours, then get up and stand another six-hour watch. The two people who stand the "port & starboard" watch are usually "hot racking", which means that they share a rack. It's called "hot racking" because when one person is sleeping the other is on watch, so the rack is always warm. That thought gives me the willies.

In the past four days, my body has finally begun to adjust to the life cycle at sea. I am in training now for standing my first watch in the back aft area that houses the reactor compartment and engineering spaces. For security reasons, I can't be specific about what is back there, but generally, it's a steam plant that drives turbines for electricity and the main engines for propulsion.

Battleship gray is generally the color of the equipment, which makes an interesting contrast to the Sea Foam Green that covers the rest of the bulkheads, piping and conduits. The maze of conduits, cables and piping completely take over the overhead and then eventually snake their way down to either some type of equipment, device or to the many bilges below the deck plates. Steam piping can be distinguished from the other piping by its thick layer of insulation. Steam valves are also wrapped with thick blankets of insulation to cut down on the amount of heat produced by the steam generators reaching the engineering spaces. The temperature in the engine room, while steaming underway, fluctuates from 90 to 100 degrees, depending on how deep the boat is and what waters she is sailing in.

Air-conditioner ducts criss-cross in the overhead and drop down to provide little pools of cool relief from the heat and humidity. Deck plate walkways apparently added as an afterthought, since they zigzag a path up, down and around the turbine generators and the main engines. One deck plate pathway ends right in between the main engines, the hottest accessible place on the boat. Often people, like the XO, will run in place there to take advantage of sauna- like conditions.

All the way back in the aft of the boat are the shaft, a couple of workbenches and an emergency propulsion machine.

The coffee mess sits just outside of Maneuvering and is normally maintained by the Auxiliary Electrician Aft (AEA). It is the AEA's duty to rove the engineering spaces, since other watch standers aren't allowed to leave their assigned areas. When they need coffee, they growl "Maneuvering", through the ship's communication system (2JV).

Built on the science of two tin cans and a string, the 2JV is the sub's main communication device. Its hinged mouthpiece of is mounted on a breastplate, along with a set of headphones. A button on top of the mouthpiece, when depressed, allows the phone talker to communicate with others on the line. Anyone who picks up a handset on the 2JV phone line can be heard by anyone else, like a party line. Think Sherriff Andy Taylor from Mayberry on the phone. A cloth strap fastened at the top corners of the breastplate secures the 2JV around your neck. Central locations throughout the boat have gray rectangular boxes, called "growlers", which are about the size of a box of macaroni, equipped with a phone handset and a plug-in jack for a headset. An AM-radio-type speaker fills up the left side of the box. Just to the right of it is a selector dial used to "growl" other growler stations. This is accomplished by using a hand crank on the right side, which generates a growling, chirping noise at the station selected. Once again, Andy Taylor had to crank the handle to get Sarah, the telephone operator. With this device, a watch stander could communicate with practically any one else in the boat, whether or not any ship's power is available. In addition to the growler stations, peppered throughout the boat are individual plug- in jacks, available for casualties or special operations.

The last time I was standing my training watch (was it just 12 hours ago?), there was a discussion about the movie "10". The general consensus was that people went to see Bo Derek naked, but left the movie talking about how hilarious Dudley Moore was. Just the thought of him outside, talking on the phone and eventually falling down the hill still makes me laugh. And, although some would disagree, I think it was the perfect date movie.

For example, a girl might ask her boyfriend to take her to see "10". He thinks "Oh wow! Yeah, Bo Derek". But there is a convoluted moral to the story showing that bad things can happen if someone decides to cheat. The fact that Dudley Moore and Julie Andrews were not exactly married, solidified the theory, because everyone still thought he was cheating. Sure, he was in a relationship, but he wasn't married. It can't be cheating if you are not married. Sexist, I know.

I didn't bring this up in our conversation, but I've always thought Julie Andrews was a "10", and this movie sure showed her sexy side. It must have started when I was young and first watched "Mary Poppins", with her English accent and prim and proper appearance. It made you wonder what she was like "behind closed doors", to steal a line from Charlie Rich. I'll bet it would have been supercalifragilisticexpialidocious.

Bernie Simmons, an avid (rabid?) photographer stands watch in the upper level of the engine room back aft. He'd been discussing with Electrician Mate 2 (EM2), Jake Statler, the auxiliary electrician, who has been training me, that movie, Bo Derek and the whole "10" rating system for women. Bernie asked Jake who he would rate a "10" on TV right now?

"That's easy," Jake said, "Lydia Cornell, Too Close for Comfort. She wears a sweater like it oughta be worn." All I know about Jake is that he grew up in New York and belonged to a street gang. It was no big deal, he said, just a matter of survival. Everyone joined a street gang, because there was safety in numbers. He told me about a recent movie called "The Warriors", which was a little unrealistic, but the concept was still true. Instead of wearing costumes, it was more common for gang members to brand themselves in some way or to get a gang-symbol tattoo. Jake has tattoos on his arms that you can actually see because he's hairless which is the opposite of Chief Garrison. With narrow eyes set below thin eyebrows, he appeared to be frowning even when he was smiling. He had thin black hair parted in the middle and was constantly running his hand through it as he talked. Or I should say "tawked'. His accent was so thick, Archie Bunker could have been his dad.

In perfect contrast, Machinist Mate 1 (MM1) Bernie Simmons is the most laid-back person I have ever met. Nothing seems to surprise or bother him. While Jake is a tough guy from the city, Bernie was brought up east of Nashville. Not too tall, not too short, not too thin, not too fat, Bernie could easily get lost in a crowd. His face, soft and spongy-looking, seemed to always have a smile on it. The thick brown hair on his head grew like a weed and had a mind of its own.

His dad owned a local hardware store for over 30 years. Bernie showed a mechanical aptitude early on, by helping his Dad in the store, and he took that skill into the Navy. Bernie told me stories of his childhood including swimming in nearby Percy Priest Lake. He and his friends would jump from rocky cliffs that were up to sixty feet high. The lake was formed when Percy Priest Dam was built. Bernie claimed that there are still abandoned houses deep underwater in some parts of the lake, and catfish as big as cars!

The friendship between Bernie and Jake was odd. Jake, a street-gang-toughened city dweller, and Bernie, a slow-paced, small-town dweller. Here are two people from completely different backgrounds and cultures and yet, here on this sub, they have become friends. Go figure. I'm sure, if they had just met by chance on the streets of New York or maybe at Opryland, they would have barely noticed each other.

So, Bernie continued, diplomatically, " You know, Jake, I agree Lydia has two very good reasons (as he motioned with cupped hands) to be a "10", but my vote would have to go to Loni Anderson on WKRP."

Then, Burton, the Throttleman poked his head out of Maneuvering and "Hold it. I don't remember her real name, but that woman who plays Bailey is a **whole** lot better looking than Loni." Since Burton once told me he is head over heels in love with Jane Pauley on the "Today Show", Bailey was a surprising choice. Maybe he goes for the serious tom-boyish types.

Electrician Mate 3 (EM3) Darryl Burton is an overly, energetic guy from Arizona. I forget the town. Seeing that he is chubby and bubbly, he was given the nickname "Doh-Boy, from the Pillsbury Dough Boy. He is always cracking jokes or

37

telling some funny story about growing up in Arizona ("Why did the chicken cross the road? To show the armadillo how it's done!").

He has dirty blonde hair, with freckles splattered under his eyes. If there's a party with a lot of laughter, Doh-Boy will be smack in the middle of it, wide eyed, and hands gesturing wildly as though they had a life of their own, as he recreates an unbelievable story that he's heard about or experienced. Mostly experienced. Are they true stories? Maybe not, but who cares? They're entertaining.

"Sure, maybe in the face," Bernie granted. "But I'm talking about the whole enchilada, the whole package." The cupped hands gave a more definitive description.

That remark inspired a mini-discussion among us watchstanders about the comparative attributes of Bailey and Jennifer, and then flowed to the eventual comparison to Ginger and Mary Ann. However; this time, Doh-Boy added a new twist.

"How come when we compare Ginger and Mary Ann we always leave out Mrs. Howell." First there was silence, then someone laughed with a chorus of groans and remarks about getting serious, paying them no attention and going boldly where no man has gone before. Doh-Boy added, "You know, I don't think any of you have looked at her. I mean, really looked at her. If you think about it, she was the only one on that island that could actually have sex because she was married. Ginger and Mary Ann couldn't and probably wouldn't. Look at their choices. Do you think the Skipper or Gilligan had a shot with either one? Now maybe the Professor…"

"Unless Ginger and Mary Ann were with each other."

"No way."

"In your dreams."

"You bet in my dreams. They stayed in the same hut."

"So, did the Skipper and Gilligan."

"In YOUR dreams."

"Ginger might, being from Hollywood and all, but Mary Ann would never ever do that."

"How do you know?"

"Because she grew up on a farm in Kansas. Their values are different from Hollywood's."

"Hmmm…farmer's daughter…oh yeah sure. She is soooo innocent."

"Maybe you have a dirty mind."

"Guilty."

"Look, all I'm saying is that what Mrs. Howell brought to the island was civility. She was their culture. She was their civilization. If it wasn't for her, they might all have ended up like 'Lord of the Flies' or something. And she was probably a mother figure to Ginger and Mary Ann. Well, maybe mother is too strong. Maybe more like an eccentric aunt. I think she helped them to remember that they were women. They probably had long talks in the girls' hut".

"Aw right!"

"And," Doh-Boy shot Jake a dagger look, "she reminded them to be strong and not to fool around. She was charming, always in good spirits, and rich."

"And old. You into older women Doh?"

"Hey Doh-Boy, stay away from my mom."

"Too late." Doh-Boy grinned.

"I know why you like her, she's rich!" Bernie exclaimed.

"Well it's certainly in her favor," agreed Doh-Boy. "And by the way, how rich is your Mom, Bernie?"

Then Machinist Mate 3 (MM3) Charles "Chuck" Cummings interrupted, "You know, since we're talking about the whole Ginger/Mary Ann versus Jennifer/ Bailey thing, did you ever notice the similarities between Gilligan's Island and WKRP?"

"One was on an island and the other in an office. Oh yeah, rreeeeaaaallll similar." As Jake stretched out the word "real", he rolled his eyes.

Chuck is a Machinist Mate who normally stands a lower-level watch in the engineering spaces. Hailing from Chicago and more cerebral than the rest of us (or at least he gives you that impression), he's quiet most of the time and seems to observe more than participate. He is of medium height and medium build. Top that off with brown hair and brown eyes, and he could easily get lost in a crowd. He doesn't seem to have any physical features that would make him stand out. But there is one thing about Chuck that stands out. Chuck read books and lots of them. Fiction mostly.

When I passed by his room at the barracks, he'd be stretched out on his bunk reading the latest best-seller. I guess it was a best-seller. Once he proudly showed me his display rack in his closet on base. He contracted with someone locally and had it custom made out of wood, maybe oak. Especially designed only to hold paperback books, it had to be at least 10 rows high and almost as wide as the closet. I don't remember any specific titles, but there was a healthy mix of science fiction, westerns, mystery (I did see an Agatha Christie. At least it wasn't Nancy Drew.) thrown in. Boxes on the floor of his closet overflowed with paperback books, and the top shelf had boxes labeled "books".

When I asked him why he didn't send them home for storage, he said matter-of-factly that he was an only child, and

41

his parents had died in an automobile wreck when he entered high school. Drunk driver. Except the drunk was his father. As an only child, he had to take responsibility for burying his parents. Man, that had to be tough, to be fifteen years old and dealing with all of that. His uncle came to stay with him to keep Social Services from sending him to a foster home. Excuse me, his good-for-nothing-lazy-leech-of-humanity-of-an-uncle uncle.

After graduating high school and selling his parents' house, he couldn't imagine going to college, so he decided to join the Navy to get away from everyone and everything. Books, he said, were always an outlet, so, after his parents died, he read even more. Now he goes through a book in two days. When he goes to sea, he really stocks up on books.

"Hold on." protested Chuck, "and go with me on this. You got the Professor who was the smart one and people came to him for advice, but he wasn't officially in charge. That could be Andy on WKRP, Andy was also the smart one. People come to him for advice and he also isn't officially in charge. I mean, he doesn't own the station. Mr. Carlson owns the station. The Skipper was Mr. Carlson. They both were heavy-set and owned something that the others were involved in. Carlson had the radio station, the Skipper had the Minnow. "

"And Gilligan is Les?"

"Exactly!" Chuck's eyes were now dancing. "Those two were both accident-prone, the clowns of the show. Les always wore some type of bandage. Of course, Ginger and Mary Ann are Jennifer and Bailey. Now here's where it's a bit of a stretch. The closest person to Mr. Howell is Herb, although a young, poor Mr. Howell. And Herb's wife could be Mrs. Howell."

"What about Venus?" Bernie asked. "How does he figure into to this equation?"

Chuck was stumped. "Well, I don't know. They didn't have a black person on Gilligan's Island"

"Unless you count the natives."

"But they weren't black. They looked more Hawaiian than black."

"Well, I think that what happened with WKRP, was that the TV people realized that black people watch TV, too." Bernie declared. "Look at the TV schedule. Can you name me any other show on right now that has a black person in it?"

"Sure," Jake said trying to hide his smile. "Monday Night Football."

Well, that cracked everyone up. Then Mr. Galloway, who is black and the Engineering Officer of the Watch (EEOW) designated as the head honcho, and had been silent to this point, suddenly straightened up and said, "You forgot Benson."

"Oh yeah, <u>Benson</u> has a black man on it." Bernie agreed. "But wasn't he originally the butler on <u>Soap</u>? I think he quit that show and carried the character to his new show. The cool thing about Venus was that, he was like everyone else. He was a disc jockey just like Johnny Fever. They were on the same level and they hung out together. He wasn't a butler or a janitor or a football player. He just played a normal person."

"If you can call a disc jockey a normal person."

With that, Bernie brought out his grease pencil. "Ok, back to the list, who do we have so far?" He started to list the ones we named (excluding Mrs. Howell) on the clear Lexan-covered bulletin board outside of Maneuvering. For the rest of the watch, the list grew. It became quite comprehensive and included physical features as well as, well, to be honest, it only listed physical features. The illustrations were a tremendous help.

Electrician Technician 2 (ET2), Victor Harrington the Third, or "Harry" as we call him. He really hates that nickname and asks us to stop, which of course makes us do it relentlessly. The Reactor Operator said that he hadn't voted on a "10" yet. I think secretly that we were afraid he'd pick a

44

guy. Instead, he chose Cathy Lee Crosby on <u>That's Incredible</u>, a pick which would keep us guessing. Pompous and egotistical Victor is the least-liked back aft that I know of.

Mr. Galloway, the EOOW, picked the college girl on <u>Eight is Enough.</u> I don't know much about him or any of the other officers for that matter.

Electrician Mate 1 (EM1), Jimmy Lockridge ("Lock" or "Masterlock"), the Electric Plant Operator, said that we were all missing the boat when we overlooked Elaine from <u>Taxi.</u> Jimmy is a short-timer. In other words, he has almost fulfilled his Navy obligation, and will soon be returning to civilian life. He will go to Separations (Seps) when we get back from the Med in August. When he gets down to 30 days, he'll start a short-timer's chain. Each link of that chain corresponds to a day left in the Navy. Every day he will take out a pair of dikes and snip off a link.

Married with two kids, he actually misses his wife and kids when he's at sea. He threw a huge party at his house before we left on this Med Run. Or, I should say, his wife did. Most military parties consist of a keg of beer, a bag of chips and some sort of dip, bean or French onion; pretzels are optional. For this one, however; Lock's wife, Sheila, fixed an impressive spread of vegetable, cheese, bread and meat

45

platters. Of course, the prerequisite kegger was there, but that was the only resemblance to a Navy party. Besides the tasteful decorations (Wow patio lights!) and coordinated seating, there were various soft drinks for the kids and white wine for the ladies. When I complemented her on her home and party, she thanked me politely without looking directly at me. John told me later that she told his girlfriend, Karen, that she hated military life. Shelia said the longer Lock was around the military, the more bad habits he picked up. It's especially bad when he comes back from being at sea. She said he never used to cuss, and his whole attitude around her and other women has changed, almost as if he's forgotten how to act like a person instead of a sailor.

She complained that her life was constantly disrupted. It wasn't just the sailors who had to adjust to long periods of absence. She, too, continuously had to adjust her life from being in control of the family when he is away to relinquishing that control when he returns to port. She is really looking forward to his leaving the Navy in August. I said that maybe Karen was giving him subtle hints about his own behavior. He said it was possible, but then again Karen wasn't a long-term girlfriend. It wasn't as if he was going to marry her or anything. I think he cares about her a lot more than he realizes. As the third wheel on a couple of their dates, I noticed that he seemed wrapped up in her. And who wouldn't be? Karen was a natural beauty with shoulder-length shiny black hair, and a field of freckles lay beneath Windex blue eyes. Perfect white teeth flashed when she smiled, and her eyes almost turned purple. Not that I ever noticed.

Dave Jacobs "DJ" from a small town outside of Asheville, NC, growled his choice from somewhere back aft, Victoria Principal (from <u>Dallas</u>, of course). To me, that was a good choice. She was one of the "principal" reasons that I watched Dallas. I once saw a picture of Victoria Principal in PLAYBOY when she was topless, and the term, "silver dollar", popped into my head.

I'm pretty sure DJ didn't see that picture. He is the most religious person I have met so far on the sub. When he's in port, he attends church regularly and he prays before every meal, no matter how small.

You can tell that DJ spends his time outside. Sun bleached hair, farmer's tan and a slim body. Not that I noticed, but on a sub, you discover these things. Modesty is basically out the porthole.

By the time the watch was over, you couldn't even see the Plan of the Day (POD), or the Watch Bill because it was covered with different-colored grease-pencil lists, votes and a

47

few detailed illustrations. In addition to the ones mentioned above, the nominees are; Dana Something from Soap, Chrissy from Three's Company, Valerie Bertinelli from One Day at a Time, and Mindy (my pick) from Mork & Mindy. And this was just from being at sea a few days! The only girl from Charlie's Angels that made the list was Farrah Fawcett. Remember that commercial with Joe Namath for Noxzema! Let Noxzema cream your face" That's as far as I'll go on that one. I know I've left out a few but those stick out in my mind.

"How about Kate Jackson?" asked Doh-Boy.

"She looks like she could kick your butt. But then again, who couldn't?" Jake was quick with that type of comment.

Well, that sparked another conversation about which girl could kick Doh-Boy's butt, then degenerated to which girl could kick the other's butt and how would you stage something like that? Names for a TV show popped out. "Catfight 1981", "The Dukes of Daisy", or "Different Strokes" (yeah, I know it's already a TV show, but this one has different connotations.). That's when Bernie looked up, like threw his arms over his head, and, in his best Reverend Jim (from Taxi) imitation, muttered. "It's like a real Battle of the Networks Stars!" Jake did a halfway decent Louie and sneered, "More like the Battle of the T's and A's," referring to that Saturday-Night-Live skit of a couple of years ago. After all the votes were counted, the overall winner was Valerie Bertinelli. And I won't mention how graphic those illustrations were.

Monday 03/09/81

The topic of conversation in front of maneuvering today was "Semper Fi". Well, not really so much about "Semper Fi". It started out as a discussion about military movies. Of course, John Wayne's movies were discussed. And Jan Michael Vincent's movie "Tribes".

"It seems most of the good war movies were about the Marines." Bernie lamented.

"Who do you think did all the fighting?" said Jake.

"The Army."

"Yeah, but how do you think they all got there?"

"So, what. We are a taxicab service now?"

"Taxicabs that fight."

"Oh, come on now. An aircraft carrier and a destroyer can level just about any country. Not to mention what a battleship can do." Said Bernie indignantly.

"Easy now. No one is saying the Navy doesn't pull its weight during wars. All members of the Armed Forces have a specific task in wartime and in peacetime. All branches of service are needed."

"What's cool about Marines is they have that slogan they say to each another."

"Hoo-rah?" That's a slogan? Sounds like a question".

"No. Well yeah, but I meant "Semper Fi". It's like a bond. Kind of like the wave thing that motorcycle guys do."

"We should have our own saying."

"We do. 'Peace through Science'."

"Oh boy." Jake rolled his eyes. "Yeah, I can just see us passing each on the street, saying 'Peace through Science' and then flashing the peace sign."

"We are Marines actually. SUB-marines."

"Oh, so we are below-par now?"

"Well, below sea level anyway. We go places marines won't go. Besides, we have something no other service has. Dolphins."

"The Navy's slogan is 'Not for self, but for Country'."

"But we should have something just for submariners."

The EOOW, who had been listening, spoke up and said," We do, guys. The official submarine slogan is 'Any Time. Any Where. Always Ready. Always There.'."

"Kinda long. Maybe shorten it to 'Any Where."

"That makes us sound like a shipping company."

"How about 'Run Silent. Run Deep? The first guy could say 'run silent' and the second guy could respond with 'run deep'."

"What if there are more than two people? It could get mighty confusing with who says what."

"And it would sound like a beer commercial."

"Ain't no slack on a fast attack."

"But we leave out the boomers then. It needs to include all who serve on a sub."

Suggestions were flying in now.

"can I buy you a drink". That's a line. Not a slogan.

"one boat. One crew. One shaft. One screw."

"How about Screw This."

"How about just 'Can Do?"

"Well we all can do-do."

That got a chuckle, snort and a guffaw.

There were other suggestions that included "Emergency Blow" ("Use that for when you get back home after being at sea for three months!"), "All Ahead Flank" (Surface ships do that too), "Down the Hatch" (again. Beer commercial), and "Feather the Planes" (Too obscure. Besides very few of us actually get to drive the boat.). Each one had a definitive detraction that ruled it out of use.

Then Bernie offered. "Maybe it can be an acronym. You know how the Navy has one for everything."

"Like FUBAR."

"IAW"

"OBA" "PMS" (which has nothing to do with women issues) "POD" "LES" "UA".

"WTB"

"WTB? What's that?"

"Where's the Beef?"

Another round of chuckle, snort and guffaw.

It seemed everyone came up with a good example. Until…

"EOOW." Said the EOOW.

We collectively rolled our eyes.

"So, what acronym can we use?"

"Well. Let's get some words together." We pulled out the grease pencils and started brainstorming on the doodad hanging outside maneuvering. The board started to fill up as we shouted out our suggestions. Covert. Ready. Deterrent. Force. Stealth. Underwater. Field Day. Screw. Nuclear. Eternal Patrol. The 'Eternal Patrol' reference came from Thresher & Scorpion, two nuke boats who were lost at sea, but, as someone pointed out, we've lost a lot more shipmates on diesel subs.

We decided to create a tribute for the submariners who paid the ultimate sacrifice in the defense of our country.

Remember All Submariners on Eternal Patrol or simply RA-SEP. It would be fantastic to have a written record of all those who lost their lives in submarine service. Maybe have a log or book in a museum with everyone's name in it. Ellis Island has a book of people who immigrated here. I remember that last year President Carter authorized a memorial to those who died in Vietnam. We don't need to copy what they are doing, but it would be rad to do something to remember those submariners. So, just for now, we decided to say this to each other. At least for this patrol.

Saturday 03/14/81

Last week was extremely busy for our first full week under water. As you can tell from the date, it has been a few more days since I've had time to write. Qualification has taken up most of my waking hours. Training and drills take up the rest. Sleeping fills the gaps in between. Sometimes I'll get an hour of sleep, other times maybe up to four. I just woke up from what is called an "Equalizer". I slept almost eight full hours. By the way, that name comes from a deep-cyclic battery charge that we perform on the ship's battery periodically to bring it back up to its full potential.

Speaking of drills, yesterday we got quite a scare from a ship's drill that went wrong. Before I get into that, I need to back up and explain what little I know about in the Control Room. It is located just forward of the Captain's Stateroom, which is just forward, of the XO's stateroom, which is just forward of the weapons loading hatch. Just remember that the Control Room is located right under the sail (the black thing that looks like a rudder upside down), which makes sense because that's where the periscopes are. The weapons loading hatch located aft of the sail is really the entrance for getting just about anything into the boat including weapons. The two other hatches are normally secured shut and the topside watch stands duty over the weapons loading hatch while in port. The planesmen, who steer the boat, sit in the forward part of the control room, just aft and starboard of the hatch leading to the bridge at the top of the sail. Behind the planesman is the Diving Officer, who supervises the planesmen. To the left of the Diving Officer sits the Chief of the Watch, who is responsible for just about everything else related to submerging or surfacing the boat, plus communications over the 2MC, which broadcasts throughout the boat.

The ship's casualty drill was scheduled in yesterday's POD for some time in the afternoon. It so happened that this Friday was a little different from most of the other Fridays in the year, because yesterday was Friday the 13th. Normally I'm not superstitious. At least on dry land I'm not. But, if you're travelling in a black steel tube underneath the ocean, why take a chance by holding a ship's casualty drill on Friday the 13th? It's like that Jim Croce song about spitting into the wind or tugging on Superman's cape. Perhaps in our case it would be poking Neptune with a trident or something.

No one knows which drill will happen or when it will be run. It could be a fire or flood, or a hydraulic accident. Being new, I have never experienced these kinds of scenarios before. The forward guys who went to Sub School did a lot of mock drills when they were in New London. John attended one before he came on the boat. He's been riding subs for almost four years. Since Nukes didn't attend Sub School, I was a little apprehensive about what to expect from them.

My Friday the 13th started with standing watch at midnight. I say midnight, but the watch actually starts at 2330. Midrats are served at 2300. I am now qualified as Auxiliary Electrician Aft, a relief to Doh-Boy, because he had been standing "port and starboard" Throttleman watches. My qualification allowed Jake to move off the watchbill as AEA and on to it as Throttleman. After finishing that watch at 0600, I ate breakfast and then read until the 3-hour "Field Day", scheduled for 0700. This field day is different from a field day held in school. Field day on the sub is to clean up the boat and the only way to get out of it is to have a chit or bed pass for sickness or injury. Lack of sleep is not an acceptable excuse. After the field day, the line outside the two shower stalls was long. Amazingly enough, two shower stalls normally sufficed on any given day except field day. Of course, these shower stalls are not ordinary shower stalls. Made of stainless steel and the size of a photo booth, the

57

shower stalls are situated on either side of a common area, with a sink and mirror which is useless because it's normally steamed up from constant showers. We make all our potable water on board, so there is a 90-second water- usage limit per person per shower. The theory is that, upon entering, you use about 30 seconds of water to wet down. Then you lather everything you can for as long as you want. To rinse, you use the remaining 60-seconds allotment of water. Because of the long line from Field Day, I didn't finish my 90-second shower until almost lunchtime. For lunch, Tony had cooked up a fine Navy meal of macaroni and cheese, Navy beans and "Biologics", a term given to seafood, which is what sonar men call background noises they hear in the ocean. The seafood this time was fried shrimp, and it was great. No Red Lobster, but there is no take-out service here. There is no real limit to how much you can eat, and since I was extremely hungry from the Field Day, I made sure I…uh…didn't hurt Tony's feelings.

I had been up since midnight, so after finishing lunch, I headed back to my rack to get as much sleep as I could before my next watch at 1800. After that big meal, it didn't take me long to crash. Unfortunately, it didn't take long for the drill to start. It seemed as though I had barely closed my eyes, although I do remember something about a chocolate honey-dipped doughnut from Dunkin' Donuts, when "FIRE IN THE GALLEY" came over the 2MC, followed by the ship's casualty alarm. Groggily I rolled out of my bottom rack only to have my hand stepped on by the guy getting out of the middle rack opposite me. A mass of bodies was tumbling out of their racks all around me, struggling to get dressed. Sort of like guys trying to get dressed for gym in the aisle of a school bus. Since I was already dressed, I hurried down to the mess decks and saw a Chief with a "MONITOR" badge waving a red rag over the big stainless mixer in the Galley. Since it was my first drill, I was a little apprehensive about what to do. Fortunately, a first-class torpedo man named Louis something had taken control. He turned around, saw me and shouted, "You! Get an EAB on and man the 2JV!" A couple of guys were pulling Emergency Air Breathers (EAB), out of a storage locker in the starboard wall of the mess decks. They looked like scuba masks with quick-disconnect hoses attached. The hose plugs into various EAB air stations located throughout the ship.

I grabbed one, put it on and fumbled with the latch on the aluminum storage box that houses the 2JV. I could feel the sub taking an up angle as the 2JV tumbled onto the deck.

When the EAB and 2JV were finally in place, I moved over to the passageway by the ice cream machine in the aft part of the mess decks near the TDU Room, trying to stay out of the way. Louis was yelling at two guys with fire extinguishers to stay put because of the simulated smoke (a Drill Monitor waving a large gray cloth with "smoke' written on it). Then he turned to me and said, "Tell Con (Control Room) that Petty Officer Duncan is in charge at the scene and that the fire appears to be coming from the Galley mixer." He had to repeat it twice before I got it right and then regurgitated (probably a poor choice of words being on the mess decks) the info to the Chief of the Watch (COW) in the Control Room. By then, Petty Officer Duncan had instructed one of the guys with the fire extinguisher to don a portable oxygen breathing apparatus (OBA), after which he grabbed a fire extinguisher and headed into the galley.

An OBA looks like a deflated black life preserver with a hollowed-out chest area. Two hoses that look like vacuum cleaner tubes came out of the chest area into a full-faced mask with adjustable straps like a scuba-diving mask. A green canister as big as a hard-cover book was inserted into the hollowed-chest area, secured by an arm that swings down. On the bottom of the arm is a knob used to force the can up into a pin in the hollowed-out area. That pin pierces the top of the canister and forms a seal. The warm, moist air from breathing activates a chemical process in the canister, producing oxygen. This chemical reaction produces heat, but it's safe, as long as the canister is in the housing.

After ensuring that the circuit for the mixer was de-energized, the guy in the OBA pretended to discharge the fire extinguisher in the direction where the Drill Monitor was waving the red flag. After the fire was extinguished, the guy in the OBA told PO Duncan that the fire was out. During this whole time, the sub headed up to periscope depth in order to ventilate the boat. I passed the word to the COW that the fire was out, the 2MC announced, "The fire is out. Prepare to ventilate the boat."

Down on the mess decks, as we wrapped up the simulated drill, and stowed away fire extinguishers, EAB's and 2JV's, the USS Lapon extended her diesel snorkel mast and fresh air was sucked in to dissipate any residue of simulated smoke. Another announcement noted that the drill had been secured and the drill monitors should meet in the wardroom for a critique. Crewmen slowly left the mess decks, heading forward to their racks or whatever they were doing as the boat took a downward angle. Since I was new, I was having a tough time stowing away the EAB and 2JV and was the last one on the mess decks.

The mess decks can be accessed from three directions on a Sturgeon-class, fast-attack submarine; forward, aft and by ladder from the level above. Walking back to the aft part of the mess decks, I was heading down the ladder to the laundry room when I thought I smelled real smoke. As an electrician, or "Sparky", I knew what burning electrical insulation smelled like. But that wasn't it. It smelled more like burning plastic gym socks. I sniffed around until I stopped in front of the TDU Room. The door was shut because of the garbage smell. As I slowly opened it, smoke curled around the edges of the door. One of several bags of garbage was almost completely engulfed in flames. I yelled out, "Fire in the TDU Room!" Well, that's what I meant to yell out. Actually it came out more like, "Sm...Smoke....Flames ....Flire...fire!...Down here!...Garbage place!...TDU Room"

Tony came around the corner, saw the fire, said something in Italian and then left. I didn't know where to find the closest fire extinguisher, so I tried to smother the fire with another bag of garbage. Wrong move. There apparently was some oily substance in it and the fire latched onto it. When Tony returned with a fire extinguisher, he now had a fire almost twice as big before. He told me to inform Control and tell them we had a fire as he pointed the nozzle down and activated the extinguisher. When I reached the mess decks again, I growled to the COW that there was a fire in the TDU Room. He was a little confused at first, because the drill

62

was supposed to be "Fire in the Galley". When he understood that this was not a drill, he made an announcement over the 2MC. Once again, the mess decks started to fill up, but, by that time, Tony had put the fire out.

Romanowitz a sonarman, I think, said to Tony. "We wouldn't have had a fire if you didn't use so much grease in your cooking."

Tony with a smile retorted, "I use less in my cooking than you use in your hair!"

The whole cycle started again, with the up angle to periscope depth, the snorkeling and mass of people in the mess decks. An OBA canister was determined as the cause of the fire. Apparently, after it was used, someone simply threw it in the TDU Room. Whether it was the guy who used it or the guy who stowed it away, I don't know. Those suckers get red hot when they're mishandled. The COB promised OBA training next week for the whole boat. Then he turned around, and saw me and said, "Non-qual, clean up this mess in here."

By the time I got it cleaned up, it was almost dinner time or should the last big meal of the day be called supper? Maybe it's a cultural thing. Or maybe you eat supper at home and go out to dinner. People say, "What's for dinner?" and "What's for supper?" Are they both, right? I've been up almost 18 hours with a 6-hour watch ahead of me. Might as well catch a few zzz's before watch.

Walking back to the Bow Compartment to my rack, I overheard Tony talking about Hardee's outside of the head. He shook his head and remarked, "Here I am just ten days out at sea, and I got a craving for a steak biscuit like you wouldn't believe."

"I know what you mean. I want a Pepsi." someone else said. "A real ice-cold can of Pepsi. And I hear they don't serve their soft drinks cold in Italy. Hey! (banging the stall door) Courtesy flush in there."

"Come to think of it," I agreed. "I'd like a fresh Kit-Kat Bar."

"Oh, yeah no wait, Snickers."

"When they're fresh, the chocolate is creamier and it's crispier, too."

"Crispier?"

"You know, it snaps when you break it apart."

"Same thing for a Pepsi. If you get a fresh Pepsi, it tastes crispier."

"Man, when you say crispy, I'm thinking fried chicken."

"What makes you crave something? My wife craved Chinese food when she was pregnant."

"Maybe it's a deficiency of a vitamin or chemical in your body."

"I don't know. Sometimes she would throw it up right after she took a bite."

"Maybe the father is Chinese."

"Ha Ha"

"Well, I think it's gotta be a deficiency of some sort. There are times when I will really crave real mashed potatoes with a big pool of melted butter in the middle. That's bound to be a carbohydrate addiction."

"So, craving a thick T-bone steak would be a protein addiction."

"Don't talk about a steak. It's been ten days."

"I've gone longer than that without a steak."

"Yeah, but even if you wanted one, you can't just go to Winn-Dixie and get one. The point is, we can't have one now. There is no Winn-Dixie. No Taco Bell. No Kentucky Fried Chicken."

"No Quarter Pounder with cheese?"

"With extra pickles?"

"I'll take a beer." John said as he came out of Stall #1.

"Which one?"

"Right now, it wouldn't matter much. Just give me one. Oh, and some pork rinds," he added with a grin.

"And a basketball game. March madness is going on right now and we don't even know who's in what bracket."

"So is Spring training. Baseball season will start before we reach La Maddalena."

"When will that be?"

"Well, I hear we stop in La Spezia first next week."

"Do you think they'll have a McDonald's?"

"I just hope they have beer."

"And women."

"And candy bars."

"Hey now, bars are where you'll find the beer and the women."

There was some hearty laughter and a few slaps on the back as we went our separate ways. I headed back to the Bow Compartment to my personal locker at the foot of my bed. Before we left, John had advised me to stock up on things I would need. Actually, more like making sure I had enough of the things I would want while underway. Personal effects like shampoo and deodorant were no problem. Trying not to eat all at once, the treats I have stowed away in this locker takes discipline. Rationing becomes, for me anyway, reward-based. If I got an honest sig on my Qualification Card, that might warrant a Kit Kat Bar or maybe a bowl of Cap'n Crunch. A sleaze sig may be only worth a piece of Wurther's butterscotch candy or a cup of blackberry tea. Hot tea became my beverage of choice while I was in Nuke School in Orlando. Actually, a lot of people drank tea instead of coffee to keep awake and often we traded our favorites among us. Some of the favorites, besides blackberry tea, were Constant Comment, Lemon Lift and Red Zinger.

Cigarette smokers at sea have it much rougher. They have to guess how much they will smoke before they get into the next port. They really have to learn how to ration themselves. And God help them if they miscalculate. In fact, there are some non smokers who'll bring cigarettes to sea just to sell to those desperate smokers who've run out. I've heard stories of cigarettes selling for up to a buck apiece! Geez, you can get a whole pack for fifty cents!

In my locker, I took out a Kit Kat Bar and carefully unwrapped it. Just one section would suffice for now. Putting that section between my teeth, I carefully wrapped up the remaining three sections. At that moment, someone's propped-up rack fell or a deck plate dropped or something and made me bite down on the section in my mouth, and the rest of it fell to the deck. Following the five-second rule, I quickly scooped it up, brushed it off and plopped it in my mouth.

After supper (dinner?), I headed back aft with a fresh cup of Navy coffee to stand my next watch. The coffee cups on subs are white with two green stripes near the rim, the top one a little thicker than the bottom one. Made of some type of glass, it held everything we drink; coffee, powdered milk which is now called "plastic cow", bug juice or even soft-serve ice cream. The Wardroom has real clear glasses like the glasses normally seen in a diner.

Eating is not allowed back aft, but occasionally ice cream will make it back there in a coffee cup. Cup holders are strategically placed in the engineering spaces and, depending who is on watch, the cups will be stacked two or three deep. I say that because not all submariners drink coffee. The saying that a sailor has a "woman in every port" has yet to be proven, however, the phrase "he swore like a sailor" is pretty much true. Although I have not included the swearing in this journal, meaningful cursing on a sub is a talent that has to be admired. In fact, there should be a blank and a sig needed on a Qual Card for the ability to swear like a sailor. Once a Ship's Qual Card has all the required signatures, then the prospective non-Qual goes before a Board comprised of officers and senior enlisted men. Imagine the questions he would be asked to check out his skill level in swearing.

"OK, Petty Officer Non-Qual, you have returned back to Norfolk after being at sea for a five-month Med Run. Since you are married, you know you won't have to stand duty the first day in port. You are packed and ready to go and, as soon as the brow is in place, you leave the boat for two days of stand down, looking forward to a lot of R&R, or I&I".

"I&I?"

"Intoxication and Intercourse. Your wife, girlfriend, whatever let's say both, meet you on the pier and tell you they bought something flimsy together and can hardly wait to show it to you. They pick up your bags, you put your arms around them and start down the pier. At that moment, your LPO hollers for you to get back to the boat. You find out your liberty has been cancelled because Rear Admiral Fartblower wants to tour your boat. The only problem is the Rear Admiral is in New London and can't travel because of an ingrown toenail. Therefore, the boat has to immediately depart to New London, with field days scheduled for each day of transit.

You can list the curses you would use to express your displeasure."

I'm sure you get the picture. But don't get the wrong idea. This journal is not intended to criticize the submariner. Actually, the direct opposite is true: submariners, sailors and

69

the military in general have been criticized enough. Some may be warranted. When an eighteen-year-old kid who's away from home for the first time with some jingle in his pocket and no supervision well, of course things will happen. Not all negative, but not all good, either. On the front lawn of a house in Norfolk, there is a sign that says, "DOGS AND SAILORS KEEP OFF THE GRASS." Obviously, this home owner has had some run-ins with the wrong type of sailor. But the same could be said for college kids. Or Yankees. Or foreigners. Away from home, on their own with little supervision, same stuff happens.

One of the big differences between college and the military is the commitment made by the military personnel. The drop-out rate in the military is many times lower than that of college students. The men and women of the military voluntarily make a commitment to serve their country and in return receive training that hopefully will be beneficial to them when they get out of the service. Often, they will continue their education to get a degree.

The amazing thing on subs is the close-knit feeling that permeates the crew. No, I'm not talking about the "120 sailors when they go to sea and 60 couples when they get back in port" cliché. But a real camaraderie in knowing that there is a job to be done, and it makes no difference whether the guy working beside you patching that leak is rich or poor, Republican or Democrat, black or white, nuke or forward puke, rebel or Yankee. You could be in the middle of huge argument when a casualty happens, the training kicks in and the guy you were arguing with could now be giving you orders and you obey them because the main purpose is to keep the bubble steady and the screw turning. As the saying goes, "One Boat, One Crew, One Shaft, One Screw."

Time to get off the soap box. Don't misunderstand me, I am not a "lifer-dog". The military is not my personal goal. Using the training and knowledge I have gained here, I hope to land a high-paying job somewhere with a big fat expense account when I get out in four years, two weeks, five days and a handful of hours from now.

Back to coffee cups. Many chiefs and others have their own coffee cups, almost black on the inside with coffee stains, and are **not** to be washed out. As Chief Garrison pointed out, "It took me years to get this cup seasoned. Don't even think about cleaning this cup." His is khaki colored and almost twice as big as a normal cup. Huge black letters circle the cup, "Life is too short to drink bad coffee". There are quite a few Navy- or submarine-themed cups, made of all sorts of materials, even stainless steel.

It was 2330 and I had just been relieved from watch. A thought flashed through my mind that there were only thirty minutes left of Friday the 13th. If I could just make it to my rack! The theory is that, after each watch, the most junior person of the off-going watch will take the dirty cups back to the mess deck to be washed. At times, the number of cups far exceeds the balancing skills required for one person to transport them to the Galley. So, the next most junior person in line will assist. In this case, I had to enlist Doh-Boy's help. Let me tell you, we had cups stacked and hooked and dangling all over us. Doh-Boy even had a few stuffed inside his shirt.

"Hey, don't worry." he assured me. "They're getting washed anyway."

As he headed through the Reactor Tunnel Hatch to enter the forward spaces, he tripped. In an effort to catch himself, he flung his arms out at both sides, his fingers searching frantically for something to grab on. But no luck. As he tumbled from the hatch down the step leading to the main passageway, it was like watching a movie in slow motion, sort of like Evel Kneivel missing that jump in Vegas. Evel flipped over his handlebars and landed flat on his back. His body looked like a disjointed rag doll.

Coffee cups spun off from his body in all directions like a box of burning bottle rockets, exploding on impact as they collided with various pieces of equipment. When time caught back up with us, he was lying flat on his back with bits and pieces of shattered coffee cups still spinning and wobbling on the deck around him. At first, Doh-Boy's eyes were closed, then they flinched twice and opened. And that's when I saw the blood.

A dark red pool was forming underneath his left arm. I yelled out, "Doh-Boy, you're bleeding, man! We gotta get you to the Doc!" About that time, Morris, a radioman, stuck his head out of the Radio Room and said, "Oh, man gross", but he wasted no time in getting over to us.

Morris and I slowly helped Doh-Boy sit up. Blood was streaming down from a nasty-looking cut on his forearm. The cut was about six inches long and looked deep. We checked him over and didn't see any other major problems, so I pulled a rag out of my back pocket and tied it tightly around his upper left arm. Morris clamped his hands around the cut to stop the bleeding. Doh-Boy's face was chalk-white, and his eyes were glassy.

People were gathering in the passageway, someone said he was going to get the Doc. Tony rushed up the stairs with a bag with plastic containers of flour and cayenne pepper.

I asked, "What's that for?" and he replied, "My emergency kit. It'll stop the bleeding."

He opened the bag of flour and asked Morris to remove his hands. As soon as Morris released his clamp on Doh-Boy's arm, blood again flowed freely out of the cut. Tony poured the cayenne pepper directly onto the wound and topped it with the flour. As with any deep cut, anything put on it, even water, stings like fire. So, I turned my head, winced and waited to hear Doh-Boy's screams of agony. Nothing, not even a whimper. I thought, wow, Doh-Boy is a lot tougher than I thought!

"Hey," Doh-Boy exclaimed wide-eyed. "That didn't sting!"

"Nope, it shouldn't. And, see, the bleeding's stopped." Tony said with obvious pride.

Sure enough, the blood that had been running freely down Doh-Boy's arm just a few seconds earlier had stopped cold. It wasn't even oozing when Doc arrived with sleepy eyes and an expressionless face and asked to see the wound. Don't let that expressionless face fool you, though. Doc has ridden subs for eighteen years and has seen a lot of stuff, broken bones, missing fingers, flu, venereal diseases, burns, there's not much that he hasn't come across. Although he is a Corpsman and not a bonafide doctor, he has earned the trust

74

and admiration of all the crewmen he has treated. When it comes to doctoring, he is all business. When he is not doctoring, he is one of the biggest health fanatics on the boat.

While in port, I watched him join the XO on his morning jog from our slip at D&S Piers. Doc has a neatly trimmed beard, speckled with gray and reddish-brown hair. His neatly trimmed brownish-red hair, even though it's thick, barely moves when he jogs. The XO's hair is nearly the opposite. Obviously, it's short, but that's where the similarities end. The XO's hair is jet black and what is long enough to comb is held in place by way too much Brylcream or maybe Vaseline.

From my observations during the past month, and from what I've heard, the XO is a humorless man who revels in following Navy regulations to a "T". It makes no difference whether we're at sea or in port. While in port during muster on the pier, his eyes clearly show his pleasure as he addresses the crew about the Plan of the Day (POD). When he has to relinquish control of the proceedings, he tries in vain to hide his resentment to the person who has taken over. And if that person happens to be Captain Jack, his jaw flinches while his eyes squint in an apparent attempt to vaporize the Captain. Since Captain Jack is more of a "player's coach" for the crew, the Captain and the XO have butted heads on more than one occasion. Since the Doc and Captain Jack are frequent golfing partners, the Doc sometimes acts as a buffer between them.

It seems that the only bond between the XO and the Doc is their mutual love of jogging, vitamins, healthy eating and all that crap. Don't get me wrong. They say the foods they eat and the exercise regime they follow will extend their life span. It's just that so much is given up attaining a lifestyle like that. Just the jogging alone takes anywhere from thirty minutes to an hour, not including the cool-down phase and, hopefully, a shower.

The XO is often in Doc's office talking about the latest beta blocker or enzyme that is supposed to prolong life or grow hair or increase energy. Doc appears to enjoy talking about that stuff which is surprising, I guess, because he seems pretty cool. More and more I see two people who wouldn't normally hang out with each other form friendships on a sub.

Doc examined Doh-Boy's cut, whistled softly and said with a smile, "Nice job Doh-Boy. But if you want to get out of duty, you have to try a lot harder than that. You should have done this before field day. Good thinking with the flour, Tony. Not many people know that flour is an anti-coagulant."

"Ancient Italian secret." Tony replied, in a poor imitation of a Chinaman in that old TV commercial.

Doc turned to Doh-Boy. "Ok, let's get you down to the sewing room. Guys, give me a hand."

Doh-Boy had seemed fine until he heard "sewing room". "I-I-I don't think it needs s-s-s-sew, uh, stitches, Doc," he stammered with a wide-eyed frightened look. The color that had begun to creep back in his face was now gone.

"Now, Doh-Boy," Doc began in a soft calm, voice, "You won't even feel a thing. With the drugs I've got back there, you'll be lucky to even remember your name."

Doh-Boy nodded weakly, and the guys helped him to his feet. They walked with him and helped him down the stairs to the mess decks and Doc's office. Doc slapped Tony on the back with some comment I couldn't hear, and Tony laughed heartily. About this time, I noticed the COB standing by the stairs surveying the broken coffee cups and blood spattered on the deck. He slowly lifted his head, turned to me and said with a smile, "OK, non-Qual, now clean this crap up."

It was late that morning before I got back to my rack. I'd been up for over 24 hours, from before midnight Thursday night to 0200 Saturday morning. I kept my clothes on and I crawled into my rack. I didn't stir again until they woke me for watch at noon on Saturday. Eight glorious hours of sleep. I felt like a new man.

Monday 03/16/81

I think I might have flipped out a little last night. It wasn't a pleasant feeling. When I say flipped out, it wasn't because of anger. I mean, I wasn't angry at anyone or anything. Ok, sure, I was annoyed earlier when I'd spent over an hour just trying to get a sig on my Dolphins Qual card. Hazing is part of the ritual of being on subs, like joining a fraternity in college or being a rookie in professional sports. John warned me about it, but didn't give me specific examples. He did, however, inform me of a practice called "greasing". Although nukes are not normally involved in this bizarre practice, they are not immune, either. Without getting too detailed about the actual event, let's just say it involves holding down the prospective "greasee" and using a grease gun to inject a measure of grease in a particular body cavity south of the beltline. Greasing could be caused by a variety of things, from insubordination to a first-class petty officer to acting like a jerk, or being late to Ship's Qualification. Navy's version of a Marine's "Code Red"? Nah, we're not that intense.

As I said, nukes are not normally involved in that, but there are other ways to effectively haze a nub trying to get qualified. The point is to try to be good natured about all of this and understand that it's all part of being a submariner.

I prepared myself to do a checkout with Third Class Quartermaster Harlan Lipstein on the boat's guidance systems. I figured he was the perfect choice to give me my checkout on this system for two reasons. He was qualified ship's and is absolutely non-threatening. A pair of thick, round glasses sat on top of an angular nose that started out straight out of his face and then "nose-dived" down to his lips. His nostrils were huge caverns, and his nose hairs moved back and forth when he breathed, like seaweed moving with the tide. A little shorter than me, he looks almost adolescent, and his skin has a sheen, as if he's perpetually sweating.

After explaining why I was there, he said, "Great, I was just going to do a PMS (Preventive Maintenance) on the SINS (Ships Inertial Navigation System). Maybe you could give me a hand?"

Since he asked the question with such innocence, I wasn't expecting anything. I shrugged my shoulders, nodded my head and said, "Sure, no problem."

He opened a cabinet with fake wood-grain paneling and took out an olive-green can a little bit bigger around than a handball can but about the same height. He twisted of the top, looked inside and made a face. "Man, looks like we're out of relative bearing grease." he said, as he showed me the almost empty can. "We have more stowed away in the torpedo room. The Torpedo Room Watch will know where. Just ask for a new can of Relative Bearing Grease." He turned and started removing some tools from a nearby foot locker.

"Ok, be right back." I said over my shoulder as I headed for the Torpedo Room. My stomach had done a little backflip when he said the words "torpedo room". When you hear all those stories about greasing, they always start or end up in the Torpedo Room. I have avoided it as much as possible. However, Harlan is not the type of person I would have figured to do this.

Impatient to get this sig so I could hit the rack, I didn't immediately realize Lipstein was trying to do his part in the hazing process. I am no stranger to being hazed, or hazing others. In "A" School, new guys were asked to get a "cable stretcher" when wires were cut too short or to get a bucket of voltages drops from Chief "IronButt". Of course, neither of those items existed. But unknown to me, "Relative Bearing Grease" was also one of the items that do not exist.

The Torpedo Room is directly under the mess decks in the belly of the sub. It can be accessed from the forward part through the twenty-two man berthing compartment, or from the aft by going down a ladder from the mess decks. That ladder is the one across from the TDU Room, the site of the real fire during our ship's casualty drill. Just aft of the Torpedo Room is the Laundry room and behind that is Auxillary (Aux) Machinery One, one of the areas of the boat that is John's and every A-Ganger 's sole responsibility. In fact, the "A" in the name "A-Ganger" comes from the Auxillaryman's rate.

The Torpedo Room is a little unnerving. The first thing you notice, as you look forward, is that the room seems darker and a little lower in height than the rest of the boat. It could be an optical illusion, but you'll find yourself starting to duck your head. The second thing you notice is the unbelievable number of long, slick, green-capped Mark 47 torpedoes mounted on metal racks flanked on either side of a narrow walkway. The walkway runs straight down the center of the room and ends right in front of the Torpedo Launch Console. Two thick metallic torpedo tubes, one on top of another, flank either side of the Torpedo Launch Console. The console itself is a confusion of buttons, switches, different-colored lights and warning plates. But that's not the worst. The most unnerving part of the Torpedo room is the

TorpedoMan. Or in particular a Torpedoman named Karl "Q" Hennigan.

Since Karl's room was next to mine in port, I'd once asked John if Karl got the nickname "Q" because he was queer.

John tilted back his head and laughed, "Queer? Karl?" He shook his head, "No Karl's not queer. 'Q' is not the letter Q. It's actually short for 'Cue as in Cue Ball'. As in 'bald as a cue ball'."

Well that made sense. The only hair on his head was his two eyebrows, which hung over two intimidating coal black eyes. Instead of poopie suits, he favored work pants and a clean white t-shirt topped with his dog tags hanging from a chain around his neck. His arms were covered with elaborate tattoos that looked like depicted stories if you stared at them long enough. It reminded me of Ray Bradbury's book, The Illustrated Man.

His Navy-issued webbed belt looked more like Batman's Utility Belt. A ring of keys hung from a retractable chain clipped to his belt. A studded black leather wallet was chained to another clip and stuffed into his right hip pocket. A sharpened single locking blade fit snuggly in a leather pouch attached to his belt on the front left side. The finishing touch was a stainless- steel cigarette case featuring a pair of silver dolphins mounted on the front. An intimidating, interesting character.

He had this ritual on the mess decks while others were deciding on what movie to watch. He'd take a seat in the corner and bring out his whetstone kit. Carefully he would squeeze out a single drop of oil onto a black whetstone and spread it evenly over the grainy surface. Then he'd pull out that stainless- steel cigarette case, open it and fish out a Marlboro. Next, he dug in his pocket and withdrew an old Zippo lighter, with some inscription on it that I haven't gathered the nerve to ask him about. With his right hand, he expertly flipped and lit the Zippo in one smooth motion, and then, almost as if he expected a breeze to blow it out, he cupped his hand over the end of the cigarette to light it. He took a couple of drags before he unsnapped his knife from its pouch, opened it and inspected it for any flaws. After running his finger over the whetstone, seemingly satisfied, he started drawing the edge of the knife across as though he was trying to pare the stone into paper-thin slices.

So back to my quest for Relative Bearing Grease, I took one step into the Torpedo room and scanned the room, hoping that Cue was not on watch. No such luck. I could see him up forward hunched over the Torpedo Launch Console with his back to me. Before I could take another step, he yelled out, "Whaddyawant?". How did he even know I was here? I took a couple of tentative steps and said, "I was sent to get some Relative Bearing Grease…for the SINS."

"Who sent you?"

"Lipstein, the Quartermaster."

His head dropped out of sight as he leaned heavily on his arms and sighed. "I do **not** have time for this."

By this time, I was almost behind him, still unaware that the Relative Bearing Grease didn't exist. "Uh, he said needed it for a PMS. I'm getting a checkout on the boat's guidance system." My last three words came out slowly because at that exact moment he had turned to face me, his stony eyes locked on mine. He was holding a grease gun. I think my jaw dropped to the floor. Like that big bull dog in those cartoons.

Cue shook his head and smiled, but it wasn't a pleasant smile. Actually, it looked like it almost hurt him. "I know you're a friend of John's. He and I go way back. Piece of advice. Lipstein is playing you for a fool. There's no such thing as 'Relative Bearing Grease'." His words were slow and measured. His language was much more colorful. Since he was down in the bowels of the boat, he didn't worry too much about Captain Jack wandering down here. Who, by the way, I wished *would* wander down here. Or anyone else, for that matter.

84

"Thanks for telling me." I finally managed to say.

He snorted, "Listen, tell Lipstein that I had you opening up lockers all over the Torpedo Room. That ought to satisfy him."

"That's it?"

He thought for a second as his finger fiddled with the trigger of the grease gun, "No, grab me a cup of coffee from the mess decks. Black." Then, he turned and hooked the grease gun to a fitting on one of the torpedo tube hatches.

What a relief! After bringing him coffee, I went to my rack in my greaseless skivvies to waste a little time. Then I headed up to the control room where Lipstein was waiting. Cue was right. Lipstein giggled like a school girl when I told him about my fruitless search for the grease. Then he shared his sea story of qualification which, unfortunately, included his own greasing episode. Unfortunately for me, because he seemed to relish telling me about it, including details much too gross to include here. In fact, *I* wanted to take a shower after I heard it.

Keeping ahead on ship's qualification is a huge advantage. The two big escape activities on the boat are reading books and watching movies. Movies shown after the 1800 meal with permission from the Chief of the Watch, can theoretically continue all the way to breakfast. The set-up is much like movies in high school or vacation movies at someone's house. The movie comes in an olive-drab square case with straps and buckles and the name of the movie unceremoniously stenciled in black on the front and one side. The projector is a Bell & Howell. The screen fits on a tripod marked with white reflective tape. Some big-name movies actually make it to subs several years after release. From what I'm told, the sub tender gets the prime movies. We get our choice of what's left over, as long as another sub hadn't beat us to it. "Star Wars", "Smokey and the Bandit", anything with Clint Eastwood, and "Grease" are some of the favorites that get repeated play. Come to think of it, "Grease" is probably Lipstein's favorite. Non-Quals like myself don't get a vote.

Usually, someone pulls out the movie list. Then comes a debate about which movie to watch that night. Eventually a selection is made, usually by the most senior person, or the loudest. Tonight, neither made the selection. The discussion bounced between" Every Which Way But Loose", the "Gas Pump Girls" and "The Jerk", with no strong argument for any of them.

"Clint, we gotta see Clint"

"But ya know, there's some great nudity in "Gas Pump Girls"."

"But I think "The Jerk" has some nudity in it, too."

"I don't think so."

"He's talking about the part where Martin has his pants around his ankles!"

"It doesn't matter to me what we see as long as it's not "Ice Castles" again."

"Why? Afraid of crying?"

"Afraid of getting your butt kicked?"

Cue was sitting there, with his paraphernalia spread out in front of him, not saying a word. At an opportune brief lull in this debate, Cue suggested that he'd like to see <u>Gray Lady Down.</u> The head bobbing was almost immediate and synchronized, with a few words of agreement thrown in for good measure. John came up the ladder from Aux Machinery One and slid in beside me. Then he jumped back up, grabbed an empty coffee cup, filled it with soft-serve ice cream, and sat back down. He must have just finished watch, because he smelled of diesel fumes and oil.

"Roll it!" John ordered as he stuck the first spoonful of ice cream in mouth.

"Where's the popcorn?" asked Lipstein. "I could really go for some buttered popcorn."

"You think this is frigging movie theater?" shot back Cue with a look that made you wish you had backup. Lipstein shriveled in his seat.

I had not seen this movie before, I had no idea who was in it or what the movie was about. Even if I had known, I would have probably still watched it. All through prototype training, in simulated mock-up submarines with real water-tight doors, I had no problem with closed-in, confining spaces. Never felt claustrophobic. That was about to change.

Gray Lady Down, as it turns out, is a movie about a submarine on the surface that gets hit by an oil tanker. The collision leaves a gaping hole in the engineering spaces that quickly fills with water. Watertight hatches are shut to confine the flooding; presumably sacrificing the watchstanders who were back there trying to fight the casualty. Of course, the engineering space is where I stand my watch. Charlton Heston realistically played the captain of the boat, but maybe they should have used a fake beard, because his real one was a little scraggly.

As the sub started to sink, I could feel my chest start to tighten. With no propulsion to drive the boat back to the surface, the men desperately tried blowing the Main Ballast Tanks. Normally, that makes a sub surface so fast that it catapults almost halfway out of the water. However, for this sub, with its engine room quickly filling up with seawater, it's descent only stopped momentarily before it started sinking again (just like in my nightmare!). A flood of thoughts flashed through my mind. 'They're not going to make it. They'll either die from the implosion of the sub or drown like rats. Like scared stinking rats!' Horrible scenes of the men drowning, eyes bulging, unable to breathe, raced through my mind. The feeling of helplessness, trapped in a compartment with no way out, watching as the water starts rising up to your knees, your waist, your neck, until you can barely keep your nose above water. Then, as the water slowly covers your nose, the first slug of cold seawater enters your lungs, and your body convulses. You involuntarily open your mouth to gasp for air. But, since the compartment is completely flooded, you suck a quart of seawater into your lungs. Gripped by panic and fear, you kick and claw, frantically trying to find the surface, then realization kicks in, and you know it's over. Though it took me a long time to write this paragraph, even the thoughts were shooting through my mind at ninety miles an hour. I was dizzy and felt like I was floating, not really anchored to the seat.

My eyes darted around the mess decks to see other men's reactions to this scene in the movie. They seemed fine; some even looked bored. As I looked at all the people jammed in there, I became aware of how small the mess decks actually were and how many people were crammed in there. They filled every seat, and some were standing up in the aisle. The overhead seemed a lot lower than it had earlier. The air was hot, thick and stuffy, as if the A/C had been shut off. I couldn't seem to get any fresh air to breathe. I tried desperately to suck in enough air, and then the room started to spin. I thought for sure I was going to pass out.

Even though I was sitting still, I felt as if I was going one hundred miles an hour on ice skates across a frozen lake. One slip and I would come crashing down. I fought an overwhelming urge to get up and run from the mess decks, but I didn't know why. The tightening in my chest was getting worse, and hot flashes ran through my body, making me break out in a sweat. Every movement of my head made me dizzier. The diesel fumes emanating from John were not helping. My stomach was in knots as it twisted around my heart, and flames were shooting up from my collar.

And then it hit me: I must be having a heart attack.

"Zoinks! Scooby, where are you?" John cried out.

"Rut ro, Raggy! Re're Rinking!" answered Cue.

I should point out here that watching movies on subs is a lot different from watching them in a theater. During a movie at a civilian theater, silence is expected. Since these are not first- run movies, we're usually seen them a number of times, so we make a lot of comments throughout the movie. Some are downright funny, some are crude, some are stupid.

But this time it was helpful. When John yelled, it sort of snapped me back to reality. The room stopped spinning, and I wasn't speeding across the lake anymore. My chest muscles began to relax, and I gradually breathed more easily. I shook my head, trying to shake out the last of those disturbing thoughts and took a deep breath. 'You were not having a heart attack,' I finally assured myself.

But if it wasn't a heart attack, what was it? it was gone, but it left me a little unnerved. The whole thing, from start to finish, though it seemed like an eternity, couldn't have lasted more than a few minutes. That was not a normal feeling for me. I've seen scary movies, movies about disasters. None of them, had affected me like that scene from that movie. My ability to reason went out the door. I thought I was losing my mind. No, correction. I wasn't losing my mind. It was as if my mind had taken over and I had lost the ability to control it. My mind had taken on a mind of its own.

Maybe the closest thing I can compare it to is the helplessness and panic of being an engineer on a runaway locomotive, the coal-burning type. Picture a massive black-iron locomotive spewing thick clouds of smoke and speeding across a long trestle that spanned over a canyon with a two-thousand-foot drop. Near the end of the trestle on the other side, a section of the track had collapsed. Since jumping off the train meant certain death, the only solution was to stop the train. I pulled hard on the brake lever, but it just snapped. Somehow my mind had taken on a body of its own and, laughing insanely at me, telling me that I was going to die, there was no way out. I was trapped in an impossible situation, and my mind was only making matters worse. I have never felt such fear or panic in my life. John's "Scooby-Doo" outburst had distracted my mind enough for me to regain control. And stop the train.

Feeling much better, I lifted my head and continued watching the movie. Out of the corner of my eye I could see John staring at me.

He mouthed the words 'You ok?'.

I managed a smile and nodded.

Unconvinced, he looked at me for a few more seconds and then turned his head to the screen. I suspected that John was watching me when I was flipping out and his Shaggy comment may have been designed to snap me out of it.

The extra-curricular comments continued during the movie. When they caught up with Gates, the guy with the mini-sub, he was on the beach. After he got the news, he started running down the beach and someone pointed out that men run like girls on sandy beaches. At another point of the movie, the Captain walked into the stateroom of a flute-playing officer. The obviously nervous officer made a comment about his family back home and asked the captain if he would ever see them again. Heston told him that he would.

"He's a goner," someone said.

"Yep."

"Hey! I think I saw him once in a landing party on Star Trek."

"That'll teach him to play a flute."

"That was a piccolo."

"Brian Piccolo?"

"'(sniff)...I loved Brian Piccolo.'" Someone was doing a teary imitation of Sayers from <u>Brian's Song</u>.

There was one other time during that movie when I started feeling weird again but fortunately, once again, the extra commentary by the crew in the mess decks helped to distract me.

In the movie, the radioman on the sunken sub was talking on some device, perhaps an underwater phone, trying to reach anybody out there who was listening. At this depth, none of the antennas could possibly work. So, he kept repeating the same phrase over and over again as Heston was paced back and forth through the control room.

"Any station, any station. This is Neptune, over."

I could feel my chest tightening again. Charlton Heston patiently told him to keep trying. Then the comments on the mess decks began again. I couldn't keep up with who said what, but it went something like this:

"Opening all hailing frequencies, Captain. Sending distress signal to Starfleet Command," a Lieutenant Uhura imitator said. If he didn't get the voice right, who would know?

"Captain, the dilythium crystals can't take no more," pleaded someone, doing a pretty good imitation of Scotty.

"Request permission to blow number two Sanitary Tank."

"Hey, isn't that the kid from Caddyshack?"

"Yeah, Noonan, Danny Noonan."

"Doody!!" This was when Spaulding found a Baby Ruth in the swimming pool. It didn't really apply to Danny Noonan, but it got a laugh anyway.

"Yeah. Hey, have we got Caddyshack on board?"

"A new movie? No way, but I bet the tender has it."

"Can anyone tell me why that gopher (on Caddyshack) sounded like Flipper?"

"Well, what would a gopher sound like?"

"If a gopher could chop wood…"

"That's a wood chuck."

Just then, an underwater land-slide hit the boat. Noonan started screaming into the microphone for someone to hear him.

"Hey look, Noonan's flipping out!"

"Be the Ball, Danny! Na-na-na-na-na-na-na."

"Don't worry. Your girlfriend's not pregnant!"

Then someone started singing "I'm all right", the title song in Caddyshack. We were singing, clapping and a couple of guys were dancing by the milk dispenser, as poor Danny was hauled off from his watch station. The rest of the movie didn't bother me after that. However, after it was over, John asked me give him a hand down in Machinery One.

Once we got down there, John took a quick look around to see if anyone else was there. Satisfied that we were alone, he said, "What happened to you on the mess decks?"

"What do you mean?" I was trying to dodge the question. I was feeling a lot better now, and was a little embarrassed about it. To be honest, *I* couldn't explain what had happened.

"C'mon." John persisted. "I've seen that look before. You look liked a deer in headlights. Whassamadder, your cheese slipped off the cracker?"

"What?" My eyes searched the room as I struggled for something glib or witty to say.

"You know, you tilted. Your plane stalled. Your elevator got stuck between floors." Now suddenly John was the Mayor of Clicheville. "In other words," he moved in closer, "you flipped out."

I tried to brush that off and started singing "I'm all right" as we just had on the mess decks, working in the moves of that gopher. The truth of the matter was that I didn't want to talk about it. I didn't really know how. Even now, safe in my rack with Merle Haggard playing on my Walkman, I can't put it into words. It was overwhelmingly scary. I felt like I had to get out of there or I was going to die. I just didn't know what it was that I had to do.

"Are you sure you want to leave it like this?"

I nodded my head slowly. "It was just hot on the mess decks tonight," I finally said.

"Well, let me just say this." John looked around and absentmindedly ran his thumb over a stainless-steel label wire-wrapped to a green plastic-coated valve handle. "If you ever feel like you're flipping out and I'm not saying you were," He turned to look me in the eye. "Find the biggest goofball, screw-up, mama's boy on this sub, the guy you least respect, and say to yourself, 'If that guy can make it, I can make it.'"

"A goofball." I repeated.

96

"Not just any goofball." John added. "But a real
Gaaahhh-OOOOF-bawl."

"A Gaaahhh-OOOOF-bawl." I mimicked.

"There you go. Just say to yourself, 'That boy is a
Gaaahhh-OOOOF-bawl.'"

"That boy is a Gaaahhh-OOOOF-bawl."

John reached up, and touseled my hair and said, "All right
now, how 'bout a Fresca?" Again, he saw my blank look.
"Caddyshack? Ted Baxter?"

"Oh yeah. Thanks, John"

"And don't forget this," he paused as started out the door,
"Subs are inherently safer than airplanes." He added with a
grin. "Think about it. There are more airplanes in the ocean
than submarines in the air."

Friday 03/20/81

St. Patrick's Day came and went. The first of many missed holidays. No green beer. No green skirts. No shamrocks or leprechauns. Although, to be honest, all I would normally do on St. Patrick's Day was eat Lucky Charms cereal in the morning and drink at a bar at night. Not necessarily green beer, either. The only special thing we did on the sub was to watch a movie and eat green soft-serve ice cream. No wearing green and getting pinched if you didn't. However, under-water with 120+ men didn't seem nearly as much fun as when there are girls involved.

Not to beat to death the subject of movies about submarines, but they premiered another one on the mess decks last night. "The Spy Who Loved Me", with Roger Moore, had regular-sized submarines, and a sports car that turned into a mini-sub. They even had two-man "wet subs" chasing after the sports-car-mini-sub. "Wet subs" got their name because their interior is not isolated from the sea. In fact, the men inside have to be in full scuba gear just to drive it.

James Bond movies are at the top of my list of movies to watch. Occasionally, if you are lucky, one might be shown on cable TV. So, it was a "reel" treat to see this uncensored version of the movie. One of my favorite parts is in the beginning when they run the credits. This part usually is edited on TV. Not so last night. I have always admired the way the silhouettes of the au natural ladies are filmed and choreographed with the title song of each James Bond movie. It is nothing short of genius. There is no way you want to be stuck in a line getting popcorn when a James Bond movie starts. And, although there may be one out there somewhere, I can't think of another movie that uses this particular method.

When gratuitous nudity pops up on the screen while you're at the movies with a date, you might try to hide your eyes or cluck disapprovingly and say, "Now, there was no need for that." Anything to make her think you are not some sex-driven pervert.

Because there were no women around to observe our depravity, the start of this movie was almost surreal. All eyes were glued to the screen in almost reverent silence. But, hey, the appeal, to me, is purely artistic. (And, I read Playboys for their in-depth articles!) The beginning of "The Spy Who Loved Me" is excellent, because it features women on trampolines, doing gymnastic movements that made you catch your breath and strain your eyes, (Geez, maybe I've been at sea too long.).

Boredom has led to a few pranks these past few days. About a week ago, when someone, now known as the "Mystery Growler", dialed in "Maneuvering" on his growler and then growled at them. Maneuvering would answer the growl, but the "Mystery Growler" wouldn't respond. Kind of like a prank phone call. At first, Maneuvering and Engine room upper level were the only ones to be hit. But then slowly the "Mystery Growler" began to branch, out growling at other places, the mess decks, torpedo room and even the control room. Growlers are spread throughout the boat, so it was hard to nail him down. However, it was a big mistake when he growled the XO's stateroom. The XO was asleep and did not take kindly to being disturbed. The XO's life at sea was pretty much the same as in port. At 0630 he'd rise and go jogging back aft around the main engines. Afterwards he would have breakfast in the Wardroom. On Monday through Friday, he'd head back to his stateroom, just forward of the Yeoman's office, to begin his workday. It was not by accident that the Yeoman's office was positioned this close to the XO. The primary duties of the Yeoman and the XO were to push paperwork, so, in effect, the Yeoman was the XO's secretary.

The Yeoman is one of the most powerful enlisted men on board. Our Yeoman was Willie, or "Little Willy", Huber. His name was a misnomer. He is large, and I don't mean fat. Willie is a weight-lifter and, when in port, lifted weights competitively. In fact, he won "Mr. Norfolk" last year. He asked for a Radioman when we signed up, but the Navy sent him to Yeoman school instead. An easy-going kind of guy, he accepted his role as the paper pusher for the Navy. His office is wedged between the XO's quarters and the ELT lab, was crammed full of file cabinets and drawers stuffed with paperwork. When he sits down in there, he looks huge. As though, someone shot a ray gun and miniaturized his office, or enlarged him.

Little Willie overheard the XO chew out the COB and demanded that something be done about it. In an effort to determine the identity of the "Mystery Growler", the COB reluctantly, called a mandatory meeting in the POD, for all of the crew. The meeting was scheduled after dinner since the POD was filled with trainings during the day. The mess decks were not big enough to handle the whole crew all at once, so the meeting was held in the torpedo room. Everyone not on watch was expected to be there and, if you weren't, they would send someone to wake you up. Roll was called to make sure that everyone was present and accounted for.

It was standing-room-only in the torpedo room at 1900 hours. The movie for the night was secured. It was plain to see that the men on Port & Starboard watches who would normally be sleeping now were not happy. The COB sat calmly, legs crossed, in front of the torpedo launch console. Someone made a comment about the way he'd crossed his legs, and he shot him a look that quickly stopped the scattering of laughter that comment that resulted.

The COB lectured us about battle readiness and conducting ourselves in a military manner. He said that the "Mystery Growler" was no better than the boy who cried 'Wolf'. He warned that this annoying growler might cause a watchstander, weary from the countless times he'd picked up with no one there, to ignore the 2JV and possibly miss an actual crisis.

"And an unreported flooding casualty could easily sink this boat." He somberly spoke those words, then sat down heavily on the padded green bench to let them sink in.

"Now, I enjoy a good prank just like the next guy, but this is not even a good prank. It needs to stop and it needs to stop now. The XO wants the 'Mystery Growler's' head on a platter. I convinced him that that would be impossible. We'd have to catch him in the act. We'd need two people at every watchstation, one person to secretly watch the other. We're just a few days from La Spezia. The Captain **will** back up the XO and secure liberty if this continues. I don't think anyone here wants that to happen."

There was a round of nods agreeing that nobody wanted that, and the COB ended the meeting with a surprise announcement that the Auxiliary Electrician Forward had managed to put a trace on the growler line to assist in locating the perpetrator.

After the meeting, Chuck asked my opinion of a book he'd given me to read. Almost as if he was trying to win me over to reading. This one, is not science fiction or horror, but more like an adventure. It's called <u>Horn of Africa</u> and, even though I'm just getting started, it seems pretty good. The lead character, Jeremy Nordstrand, took on a mission to save something. Tagging along is a writer named Moody who I could relate to.

"What do you think of this mystery growler thing?" We were headed up the aft ladder to the mess decks.

I glanced around quickly. "I think the XO is overreacting." I said in a hushed tone. Hey, I don't know what the XO can hear.

"Yeah, could be." Chuck agreed. "Although, that's got to be some kind of scare tactic with the trace thing."

"Well, the circuit has no real power, so, how could they?"

"By the way, there is a reason I gave you that book." Chuck changed the subject back to his passion. I'm surprised it took that long. I know he tries to talk about other things, but it seems he uses the books he reads as a reference for everything that happens. "Let me know when you finish it. I want to get your opinion on the ending."

"I already read the ending. I read it first to see if I was gonna like the book." I was just joking, but by the look on his face, you'd have thought I'd committed a sacrilege. "Just kidding." I quickly added.

The look of shock disappeared and was replaced by a friendlier one. "Good one. Ya got me." He clutched his chest with one hand and staggered back a step as if he'd just been shot. By this time, we were on the mess decks, where they were feverously trying to set up a movie. Chuck sat down next to Jake and motioned for me to sit down too. When I saw that it was Grey Lady Down again, I said I'd seen it a couple of days before and headed back to my rack. If I didn't fall asleep, I figured I could get a little studying done on some piping tabs for qualification. Piping tabs are like roadmaps for the piping systems on our sub.

I've been working on my next watch station and trying to get some sigs for ship's qualification to avoid "School of the Boat". That's mandatory study time for anyone who the COB

104

thinks is falling behind on their qualification to get their Dolphins. Out at sea it's not that big a deal. Watching movies, poker, cribbage and all of that is secured for people assigned to School of the Boat. But, in port, it's a different story. In port, liberty is secured. Which means instead of eating at a real Italian Restaurant and drinking a warm Coke, you're studying about the ship's Sanitary Tanks.

Sanitary Tanks, by the way is an oxymoron, like jumbo shrimp, pretty ugly, or military justice. There is nothing sanitary about them. Think of it as a big Port-a-Potty at sea. All of the commodes, showers, sink drains, etc. end up in one of the three tanks on board, depending on which one is in service. Now, for a septic tank on land, when-uh-let's say, organically enriched liquid in the tank reaches a certain height, it overflows down one of the perforated pipes to be dispersed in a drain field. The sub's drain field is the ocean, but because the pressure of the water under the ocean is greater than the pressure in the sub, it doesn't flow outward into the sea. The tanks have to first be pressurized with 700 pounds of air and then, by opening a hull valve, the pressurized contents of the designated sanitary tank are blown overboard.

The problem is that the commodes on a sub are directly linked to the Sanitary Tanks. As mentioned before, a ball

105

valve is used to actually flush the commode. After finishing your business, you turn a green-handled valve, much like a water faucet on the outside of the house, to add flushing water to the mixture. Then you pull (or push if you're sitting) a large three-foot handle on the left side of the commode, which opens up the ball valve in the bottom of the bowl and Viola! The substance gets sucked into the tank. That's if the tanks are **not** pressurized. If the sanitary tanks **are** pressurized in preparation for blowing them overboard, and the ball valve is opened to flush, instead of being blown overboard, the organically enriched liquid gets blown through that ball valve in the commode and, because of the two thousand pounds of pressure behind it, effectively coats anything or anyone in the vicinity. It's not a pleasant sight. The only reason I bring this up is because I just completed my checkout of this system, got my sig and tomorrow morning, we pull into La Spezia for our first port-of-call in the Med.

I got off watch at 0600 this morning, caught a quick nap, got up again at 1100 and started on my watch station quals. My checkout on the Sanitary Tanks ensures that, there'll be no "School of the Boat" for me while I'm in port!! If I was a puppy, my tail be wagging. I was one of the lucky ones who would not be on watch when we pull in. I can't wait to walk across that brow and put my feet on solid ground. And after being at sea under-water now for over three weeks, it would be great just to walk around without trying to avoid a valve or pipe jutting out to catch a knee or elbow, or ducking to go through hatches, or just to be able to see further than twenty feet.

Speaking of seeing further than twenty feet, there was one highlight for me, almost a week ago, when we entered the Mediterranean Ocean. Because of the heavy traffic of ocean vessels going through that narrow channel, the Captain had us chugging along on the surface. A small TV monitor that gets its feed from the number two periscope sits above the Fire Control Tracking Party Station to the right of the planesmen. The OOD was peering through the number two periscope when he picked up the Rock of Gibraltar. For most of the crew, this was old-hat, but for a nub like me, it was really exciting to see something in person which I've only seen in pictures before. I must have been standing there slack-jawed because DJ, who was standing beside me with the other nubs, reached over and pushed up my chin to close my mouth.

He said, "Pretty impressive, huh?"

"I didn't think they were so massive and white." I replied slowly, still dazed.

"Kinda like Doh-Boy," he added, as he gave Doh-Boy a punch in the arm. Not THE arm. A week has passed since Doh-Boy took a header out of the Reactor Tunnel Hatch and sliced his arm. It took ten stitches to sew him up and, even with that, as the Doc said, he didn't miss any watches. However, he was relieved of Field Days and PMS's. It's short for Preventive Maintenance System, which we routinely perform on our equipment. Kind of like a maintenance schedule in the owner's manual for your car.

We're expected to pull into port tomorrow at 0800 in the morning (21st) and I can't seem to sleep. Apparently, I am not the only one. It's 2230 and the mess decks are full of people. The movie ended about an hour ago, and instead of the mess decks clearing out like normal, most everyone stayed reading, talking or playing cribbage (a game I still cannot understand how to play!). The official term for this kind of unrest is "Channel Fever". However, it's more accurate when entering the channel that links the ocean to the Chesapeake Bay back home.

We'll surface in a few hours and do a surface transit into the "Golfo Della Spezia". Once we tie up on the pier in La Spezia Harbor, it's E-Div's task to bring on shore power, which is provided by a diesel located somewhere on the pier. Chief Garrison, our LPO, told us that, once shore power is brought on, liberty will then be granted for all of E-Div, with the exception, of course, of the Duty Section.

A bank representative from the city of La Spezia will come on board to exchange their money for ours. The exchange rate right now is approximately 882 lire to one US dollar. Since we will be taking care of shore power, Doh-Boy, DJ and I have given our money to John to exchange for us. John is in a different duty section than mine, and he has to stand duty the first day we're in port. Since we are so close to the town of Pisa, he told us we should take a train to see the Leaning Tower. Actually, I want to head for the first Pepsi machine and down three or four of them. There's a line in an old song called Big Yellow Taxi by Joni Mitchell that says, "Don't it always seem to go that you don't know what you've got till it's gone". Man, that is so true for me with carbonated drinks.

This will be the first trip to a foreign port for Doh-Boy, DJ and me, so we decided to hang out together. I wonder if it's true about sailors having a girl in every port. Except for the movies, it's been a while since I've even seen or talked to a girl. Or had a breakfast biscuit. Or took a breath of fresh air. Or drove a car. Or watched TV. Geez, baseball season will be starting soon. When we get back in August, football preseason will just be starting. Here's a tally of the sporting events I will completely miss before we get back into port.

- The NCAA Basketball championships, which was just getting underway when we got underway. We don't receive any scores or news until we get to periscope depth and extend the VLF antenna. The radioman prints them out on dot matrix computer paper, and then tapes it to the wall just forward of the mess decks for us to read.

- Numerous golf tournaments, including two majors, the Masters and the US Open. Since I'm from the Aiken and the Central Savannah River Area(CSRA), I've been able to go to the Masters several times and, let me tell you, that place is gorgeous! (Can real men say gorgeous?) I guess so, as long as we don't eat quiche, too!

- NFL draft

- The College Baseball World Series

- NBA playoffs and the championship game

- NHL playoffs and the championship game

- The start of the MLB season

- MLB All-Star game

- Daytona 500

- I'm sure there must be meaningful tennis tournaments, but for the life of me I can't think of one.

Since we got underway, not counting movies, I haven't heard a phone ring, a dog bark, a radio, a car horn, thunder, a doorbell or a siren. I haven't seen a woman smile, a tree, a sunset or, come to think of it, the sun, period. Besides carbonated drinks, I haven't tasted boiled peanuts, a grilled steak, a cold beer or numerous fast-food items, like a donut or a steak biscuit. Plus, I haven't taken one breath of fresh air. On an enclosed steel-black tube with diesel fuel, oil and a hundred twenty-six guys, that's plenty enough to miss. I guess that takes care of the five senses, except for touch. Maybe it's best if I don't get into the areas I haven't touched lately.

You're probably saying that I volunteered for this, and I should quit complaining. But I'm not really complaining. There are simply things that I miss. Of course, in return for giving up this much time to be underwater, the Navy is paying my way to go to these port of calls, too. So, it's a win-win situation. We both come out ahead. The Navy gets someone to man its sub, and tomorrow I get to see the Leaning Tower of Pisa.

Tuesday, 03/24/81

La Spezia was great! Pisa was great! The food was great!
Ok, it's true what they said about carbonated drinks. They are
not refrigerated, but that's ok. The few I brought with me will
tide me over until we get to La Maddelena. And I can't say
that La Spezia was great for everyone. But I am getting
waaaay ahead of myself.

By the time we got tied up to the dock in the La Spezia
and brought shore power on, it was almost 1000.
Unfortunately for us, a diesel generator, mounted in its own
enclosure on the pier, provided our shore power, meaning
that we had to station an extra phone talker to keep a direct
link to the diesel generator operator. They tell me this is not
normally how we get shore power. Normally shore power
comes from the port utility or a sub tender. It could have
been worse, however, if there was no shore power available.
Then we couldn't shut down the reactor and the nukes would
have to keep their normal sea watches while in port.

Fortunately for us, the diesel generator was operated and
maintained by EM3 Gail McLaughlin. Petty Officer
McLaughlin, (with brown hair and brown eyes, she's no great

beauty but she has dimples that take you by surprise when she laughs), is actually stationed in Naples, but is sent up to La Spezia to tend to the diesel generator whenever a sub comes in. I said it was fortunate for us, because she knows La Spezia and Pisa like the back of her hand. She knows the train schedules and speaks a little Italian. She agreed to be our tour guide to these places, and she's a woman! After being with 126 guys for three weeks, it was nice to be around a woman. Not to mention, the look in our shipmates' eyes when we told them we were going to Pisa with a woman. But, again, I'm getting ahead of myself.

A few people back aft were grumbling about how women take up shore billets overseas. Or shore billets, period. In the Navy, women are not allowed to serve on combat-ready ships. Therefore, once qualified at their rate, they can only be assigned to shore billets. Sub tenders are considered a shore billet because, for the most part, they just sit in port, unless they are relieving another sub tender so women can be assigned to them. It's as close to the action as they're going to get. So, submariners can't rotate to a tender billet.

Whether it's a sub tender or Naples, Italy, it's harder for a guy to rotate from sea duty to shore duty, because women fill up the shore billets. Thus, their angst. Maybe I haven't been in long enough yet for it to really bother me. But I don't really see how it applies to the nuclear rate. To my knowledge, there are no women in the nuclear field. There are a few women out there in left field, however. And, to be fair, that goes for guys, too.

For example, a Machinist Mate back aft with extremely hairy arms used a razor to make one of those smiley, happy faces. He shaved the hair off his forearm to make the smiley face. We dubbed him "Smiley, the eighth dwarf". He was always doing odd little things like that. One time Derek Prawley (Smiley's real name) asked me if I ever heard of someone who got away with murder. Naturally that made me a little uneasy and I said, I hadn't.

"You know, my mother has been missing for three years." He said, not looking at me. He turned his head which seemed a little large for his body, looked me straight in the eye, his blue eyes were sharp and focused on mine. Then he smiled and said in a low voice. "And they'll never find her." He turned away, lost in thought and lit a cigarette. Because I didn't know what to say, I mumbled something about being late for logs and left. He seemed to enjoy making people uneasy.

The one who really hit it off with Gail, and the reason she was our tour guide, was DJ, much to everyone's surprise, including his! As we were hooking up shore power, DJ was

114

humming a tune by Evie Tornquist, a young Christian singer. DJ told me he'll sometimes lay in his rack with his Walkman, listening to her on cassette tapes. These personal cassette players are popular on subs. There's no room in a rack for a boom box.

He said it helped to put his mind somewhere else and kept his spirits up while at sea. That seems to be true for almost everyone I've talked to so far. They all have hobbies or something to take their minds off from where they are, watching movies, listening to cassettes, playing a guitar, or even carving wood. Gary Hatcher, a Machinist Mate back aft, carves detailed boats and other figures to give to his six-year old son, Eric, when he gets back home. Eric is Gary and Vanessa's only child. When Gary's in port, he and Eric go everywhere together. He said, it helps him feel close to Eric when he's carving these things for him.

While we were getting shore power hooked up, DJ was humming a Gospel tune as he walked past Gail. Gail instantly recognized it, and they struck up a conversation about Christian Music and its artists. I must confess that I was a little disappointed when I heard she was a Christian. Purely for selfish reasons. As she and DJ were becoming acquainted, she learned that this was our first-ever port visit, and offered to give us a guided tour of the Leaning Tower of Pisa. It was just a short train ride south of here. The only problem was that she had duty today, but would be free tomorrow. We agreed to put off the trip until she could accompany us.

If you picture the Golfo Della Spezia, the (Gulf of Spezia) as a big salami pushed northward in the west side of Italy and flanked on either side by land, La Spezia would be located at the northern end of that salami. It's cool today, jacket weather, temperatures in the upper 50's with low humidity. The air smells great, fresh with a hint of a fishy saltiness, a nice break from diesel fumes and oil.

The pier we're tied up to extends southward and is easily the longest one in the bay at over a thousand feet. To the east of us is a hodgepodge of commercial ocean-going vessels, including tankers and barges. To the west are more recreational yachts and sailboats, some tied to an assortment of piers, some anchored in the harbor. Beyond the recreational boats, hills rise up suddenly, with white stucco one- and two-story houses with terra cotta tile roofs packed closely together, the gaps between them filled with small trees and shrubs. Going on the steep hill behind the homes, large white stones seem to poke through what appears to be poor-quality astroturf. The Mediterranean Sea lies just over the hill to the west. To the north and east, more city buildings surround the water's edge and, beyond them, gray-blue mountains hint at the start of the Alps.

Just northwest of the pier are other navy vessels in various sizes from different countries, some from the Italian Navy. At the end of the pier, due north, is the city of La Spezia. Since we weren't going to Pisa until the next day, we decided to explore the city and feast on its cuisine.

"Let's see if we can find a McDonald's," suggested Doh-Boy. He'd asked us to call him Darryl while we were in port. However, the first time I said "Darryl", it felt really odd so, I asked if I could shorten it to "Doh". Naturally, he gave in.

DJ said, "No way. I didn't travel this far to eat at McDonald's."

"Just kidding." Doh said half-heartedly. A quarter-pound hamburger sounded pretty good to me, actually. Strange, but I kind of wanted to find a McDonald's, too. Or a 7-11 or a Winn-Dixie. Something a little familiar. It was exciting to see something new and different, but it was also a little unnerving. We zipped up our jackets, headed down the pier, and entered the town of La Spezia.

The buildings downtown varied in height from one story to several stories high, with just a sliver of sidewalk wrapped around them. Constructed of dark brick or stucco or patched with stucco, these buildings showed their age. New buildings were few and far between. The narrow streets separating the buildings were paved with black asphalt, concrete, or red brick, or a combination thereof. Some of the streets were lined with miniature cars almost as if someone had found a way to grow a Hot Wheels car or shrink a Volkswagen. Occasionally, an American car would drive by, but it looked cumbersome and out of place, like an adult trying to roller skate with a group of children.

We were just starting to get tired of walking when we found a restaurant with one of the taller buildings resting on top of it. *Porta de Ristourante* was painted in black letters on a white wooden sign attached to flat black wrought iron. Through the windows, we could see thick dark green curtains, slightly open, hung from large polished round wooden rods. In the window next to a large aged, but well maintained wooden front door, a neatly typed menu displayed the entrees with prices listed on the right. Since it was in Italian, none of us could read it. Feeling a little brave and very hungry, we entered the small, dimly-lit restaurant.

Though it was almost noon, it was nearly empty. It had an old-age smell, like my grandmother's house. The tables were circular, with white tablecloths, making a stark contrast to the dark wood underneath. The thick wooden chairs were all tucked closely to the tables waiting to be chosen.

A middle-aged waiter appeared, his eager coal-black eyes beckoning beneath oiled jet-black hair combed straight back. His toothy smile split a thin face that sported at least a day's growth of beard hair. He was dressed in black pants, and a long-sleeved white cotton shirt. Although a little threadbare, they were clean and neatly pressed.

"Americans, no?" he asked as he directed us to a table. I wondered what had given us away. We all wore jackets and jeans because of the weather, but I thought DJ stuck out a little bit with his Star Wars T-Shirt, as though Lucas was really going to do another Star Wars.

"That's right," DJ answered. "Our sub just pulled in."

"Ah, submarine sailors! Our most favorite guests! My name is Antonio, your servant." Antonio performed a well-practiced bow. Something told me that if we'd been Tibetan Goat Herders, we'd still get "most favorite guest" status. Still, it didn't really feel insulting or patronizing.

I had my first taste of real Italian pizza, learned the meaning of antipasto, and drank my first cup of espresso, served piping hot in a thick ceramic demitasse cup with no handle. There was an antique silver bowl full of sugar, with a miniature spoon to sweeten the thick dark liquid. Because of its bitterness, it's best not to drink it black. When sweetened, espresso is a great pick-me-up after a full-course Italian meal.

119

We liked the restaurant so much we went back that night, and again when we returned from Pisa. Although we'd discovered it by accident, it was no mystery to the others, since we saw guys from the sub that night and Sunday night. In fact, that was when we found John inside plastered. More on this later.

Sunday morning greeted us with fog and slightly cooler temperatures. At 0800 we met Gail at the end of the pier for our train trip to Pisa. It was strange seeing her in civvies. She looked like a regular woman in her Calvin Klein jeans, peach colored shirt, (I'm a guy. I don't know a blouse from a camisole.) and black leather jacket. We let DJ take the lead and he started the conversation. Doh and I did a lot of smiling and nodding as they pleasantly chatted about their time apart from each other. It must have been a whole twelve hours. I knew DJ had volunteered for phone talker duty the night before, and he and Gail did a lot of phone talking.

Though it was only a short walk to the train station, we were glad we wore our jackets. The train and the station were designed differently from those back home, but the essential elements were all there. We found two pairs of seats facing each other. I sat next to Gail and we settled back for our short ride to Pisa. After a while, the coffee and fresh milk I'd had for breakfast began to churn in my stomach. I delicately excused myself to "drain the water off the potatoes" and got up to search for a bathroom. Gail smiled and pointed to indicate one at the end of each car.

A lone door in the rear of the car was marked "W.C." Not sure what that meant, I was hesitant to open it. What if it meant "Women and Children"? With the water still on the potatoes, I returned to my seat.

"You look flushed." Doh-Boy quipped. "Everything go all right?"

Looking sideways at Doh-Boy, I grinned and directed my question to Gail, "What does 'W.C.' stand for?"

"Water Closet. It can be male or female on a train," she replied.

"Just didn't want to cause an International incident." I got up once more to finish my business.

"Don't worry. There wouldn't be enough evidence to convict." Obviously, in a great mood, Doh-Boy was in rare form today. I was afraid Gail would get offended, but both she and DJ chuckled. As it turned out, I was the only one who turned red.

Once inside the cramped Water Closet, I could see it was made mostly of steel and simulated wood trim. A small shiny steel sink sat beneath a pump-action faucet neatly tucked diagonally in the corner opposite from the commode. It all reminded me of the head on the sub.

When I lifted the lid to begin draining procedures, I was surprised to find that there was no bowl. Just the ground rushing by. Now, out in the country-side, this is probably not a problem, but what do they do when the train passes through a city? At least, with all that air rushing by, the water closet was well ventilated, so there'd be no smell emanating throughout the train.

The rest of the trip was without incident, and we arrived at the train station in Pisa on time. Not to beat a dead horse about bathrooms overseas but, when we disembarked from the train, I decided to check out the head at the station. It's not easy to urinate while being jostled about. Just about the time you get relaxed enough to go, the train hits a bump or a gopher or something, not to mention that it's gently rocking from side to side. Trying to maintain balance and correct aim, while hoping no one knocks on the door is not conducive to a productive completion. And sitting is not an option, are we not men? However, the bathroom at the train station was even more primitive. There were no fixtures to speak of. Just a hole in the floor like a drain with a flushing valve above. Good thing I didn't have to go, mostly.

It was just a short taxi ride from the train station to the front gates of the Cathedral Square, also known as Piazza Del Duomo, where the Leaning Tower of Pisa is located. By the way, do not call it the Dynamic Duomo. They will not get the joke, trust me.

Think of this place as the entrance to an amusement park. In fact, parts of it reminded me of Disney World or maybe Epcot. A high red brick wall surrounded a huge courtyard, much bigger than a football field.

Once you pass through the large iron gates, the first thing you see is in the distance is the Leaning Tower, just slightly off center to the left. The inlayed-stone road runs straight from the entrance gate. A row of huge white-painted chained concrete bollards, about three feet high and a good twenty-four inches in diameter, lined the left side of the road, protecting an expansive manicured lawn in front of three beautifully ornate cathedrals. The bollards, spaced about four feet apart, reminded me of the old-style clothespins before they had a hinge. The cathedrals were white with intricate patterns cut into the stone. The two front doors, twelve feet high and five feet wide, on one of the cathedrals were completely covered in bas-relief, depicting, I assume, religious scenes.

On the right side of the road, it was more like a carnival, with a row of booths selling everything from Leaning Tower of Pisa post cards to tiny Leaning Tower of Pisa night lights. DJ and Gail decided to check out the cathedrals, while Doh-Boy and I checked out the booths.

After picking up a couple of souvenirs, we made our way through the maze of people taking photographs of them holding up the Leaning Tower and reached the entrance to the tower itself. After climbing the seemingly endless circle of stone steps to the top, what got my attention there, was the thin, frail looking pipe rail that was supposed to keep people from doing a header off the Tower. I was afraid to even push on it. As I looked over the leaning side, I felt the urge to jump. It was almost surreal. I felt that I wouldn't get hurt. Kind of like falling in a dream. It lasted only for a second, then I felt creeped out.

Once we were back down on Mother Earth, we met up with DJ and Gail and headed over to a restaurant almost directly across the street. Occasionally, I would look back over my shoulder at the Tower while we were sipping sweet red wine and nibbling on cheese and bread. I half expected to see it topple over, or someone fall off the top, pieces of broken railing tumbling down with him. Of course, nothing actually happened, except for the pleasant buzz from the wine.

After a while, Doh-Boy and I split off from DJ and Gail. They weren't paying too much attention to us anyway. We caught a taxi back to the train station and took the next train back to La Spezia.

Wednesday, 3/25/81

Today I realized that I never got around to
telling what happened to John on Sunday. I mean, finding
him drunk and bleeding at *Porta de Ristourante* Sunday
night. To better explain what happened, I have to go back
to Saturday afternoon, the day we pulled into La Spezia.

Doh-Boy, DJ, Gail and I had already left on
our tour of La Spezia. The duty crew, left on board to
load stores and tend to the ship, were wishing they didn't
have duty when the boat pulled into port. The one good
thing about having duty first is being able to read the mail
that had accumulated over the last two weeks.

John had told me about the great letters
Karen wrote to him while he was at sea. He didn't go
into great detail about the actual content of the letters,
only hinted that this one was about her taking a bubble
bath or, well, never you mind what else.

He informed me even her envelopes smelled
fantastic. Before sealing them, she would spray "Wind
Song" on the pages and, let me tell you, even after a trip
across the ocean, when that fragrance reached your nose,
it made you think of her curled up on a couch by a

crackling fire with a glass of sweet red wine. Her auburn hair, perfectly framed her face, before resting comfortably on a green cashmere sweater. Her eyes, reflecting the fire, and dancing with excitement over the freckles lightly sprinkled across the bridge of her nose. Not that I'd thought much about it.

As you can imagine, John was extremely eager to get letters from Karen. The last time he had spoken to her or seen her was the night before we left. She couldn't see him off, because she had to work. Come to think of it, to really explain this, I need to go back to that night before we left on this Med Run, to a place called "The Fifth National Banque".

"The Fifth National Banque" is not a bank or "banque", with tellers, a vault and a place to deposit your money. Well, you can deposit your money there, you just don't get it back. The Fifth National Banque is a country bar on East Little Creek Road. Not really a bar, at least not like any bar I've ever been to. A fan of Country Music, I have seen many country bars and, with a few exceptions, they are pretty much the same. There's some NASCAR memorabilia hanging somewhere behind the bar of a race car driver who lives in that state. Surrounding the bar, there are at least two or three different kinds of bar stools, some padded, some not, some patched with duct tape. Hanging over the pool table is a light that features a particular brand of beer. A chunk is missing from one corner where an overly enthusiastic guy successfully double banked the eight ball. The shot was difficult to make, because the pool table has a slight break to the corner pocket, there's no chalk, and some of the cue sticks don't have tips. The bathroom has fifteen different layers of paint on the walls, floor and light switch. Of course, I can only speak for the men's room. Although once I did walk in on a woman who was worshiping the porcelain gods in the men's room at a bar in Charleston. It was not a pretty sight. I almost kneeled and worshiped with her.

The Fifth National Banque was more like "Gilley's" in the movie, "Urban Cowboy". The Banque had three different bars, with mirrors (not one was broken!) behind the bartender. The pool tables were dark green and top-notch. The huge dance floor was wooden parquet, with elaborate lighting in front of an elevated stage that didn't even have chicken wire around it. In the front, on the right, as you walked in was a country store with shirts, hats, boots and homemade crafts. The waitresses were nice and great-looking (or was it just the beer?), and Belle, the lady who ran the country store, made you feel at home. That was important. I went through two years of training away from the area where I grew up, then got stationed here in Norfolk. That feeling of familiarity was as rare as a fast-food restaurant with empty trash bins.

Before we got underway on this Med Run, John, and a couple of guys from his division, Karen and I headed to the Fifth National Banque as a Bon Voyage treat for ourselves. As usual, Rick Stanley and the Heavy Cowboys were playing, and we made our usual song requests, 'Me and the Elephant' and 'It Ain't Easy being Easy'. I knew John and Karen were going to leave us eventually, so they could have some time together, which was fine with us. After we got settled at our table and ordered drinks, John excused himself to head for the head. We made small talk while he was gone. I asked her if she knew why the Soviet spy turned red. When she said no, I said that he saw the Italian Dressing. She threw her head back, clapped her delicate hands and laughed. She had such a fine laugh. Not artificial or donkey-like, but almost musical in its tone and cadence. As her laughter died down, she met my eyes for a split second, then turned away and focused at the people line dancing on the dance floor. I don't know if it was me or what, but in that split second, there was a wealth of information that I couldn't decipher. Or, maybe I was just imagining things.

John was the leader of this group, as he usually was, so the conversation stalled in his absence. The other two guys glanced around the room for something pretty to watch while they nursed their beers. At the time, I didn't know John's friends from the boat that well. There was Larry, the taller one they called "JJ". The other guy's name was Frank or Franklin, or something like that. Then John appeared and said, "Hey guys, let's go shoot some pool."

As they were getting up, he added, "You know, you can shoot pool all your life and not be known as a pool-shooter. But just try having sex with someone's mother just once!" His voice trailed off and there was a split second of silence before the laughter bubbled up. From everyone except Karen. She forced a smile, blinked several times and nodded. Briefly her eyes showed sadness and, even though she was sitting across from me, she seemed to be somewhere far away.

The rest of the night was uneventful. JJ and Franklin (I was close!) found two loud girls in leather-fringed vests at the bar who loved having their drinks paid for.

John and Karen left around nine to head back to her apartment. I walked out with them to see them off. They looked like the perfect couple when they climbed in John's pick-up. They really dressed up. Not that they weren't country music fans, they were brought up on Merle and Conway and Loretta and Johnny, like me. They simply dressed well. It suited them. To see them otherwise, would be unnatural. From behind John, Karen waved, her eyes lit with laughter, the sadness all but gone.

As I mentioned before, when we are underway, we cannot get regular mail. Occasionally, someone would get a Family Gram, little Western Union-like messages some of the married guys got from their wives. Those messages are carefully screened by a ScreenerMan (no, I don't know his real name) before the message can be transmitted to the submariner. Although a few of the wives would tried to covertly slip in coded sex messages, like "Shaky pudding is ready" or "Peaches says hi." They knew not to include depressing news and, if the wives forgot, it was ScreenerMan's duty to prevent it from reaching the submariner on patrol. It should be called a "Happy Gram" and come with a smiley face because its only real function is to let the submariner know that everyone is fine at home, the kids are doing well in school, and the house has not burned down. Even though the opposite might be true. From what I hear, submarine wives are the bravest of wives. Besides being both the Mom and Dad at home, they have to handle all of the day-to-day details of running a household. On top of that, they never know exactly where their husbands are. If something went wrong, they couldn't tell their husbands. They had to handle it on their own.

So, John got a letter from Karen, while you probably guessed, it was a "Dear John" letter (Ironic, isn't it?). When we got back late Saturday night, John was on the mess decks. That's when he told me the news. I was shocked, because I thought of them as the perfect couple. When I told him that and said that I was sorry this had happened. He brushed it off as if it was no big deal, that women come and go when you are a submariner.

"Besides", he said with a grin. "This'll give me and Cue a chance to taste the local flavor, right Cue?"

Cue was stretched out on a bench seat, arms folded, back against the wall. He nodded slowly and pulled the toothpick out of his mouth. "It's about time, too. I never liked Karen anyway. She was always trying to change you. She made you sell your bike. And you only went drinking on the weekends because of her. For God's sake, you even put down the toilet seat! She's had you wound, wrapped and whipped, but, Buddy, not any more. It's time you and me did some serious partying." They high-fived, as though they'd just scored a touchdown and laughed a little too long and a little too loudly.

No doubt Cue had made the speech before and, more than likely, the partying he did would be anything but serious.

John smiled and shouted, "Yeah man!" or something similar to it. But even though his face was smiling, his eyes were not.

Early Sunday morning, we went on our way to Pisa. John and Cue went on their way to party. Two groups of people headed off to do opposite things. We were going to take in the local culture and be civilized. They were going to take in the local fermentations and be well, uncivilized.

After our trip to Pisa, we got off the train in La Spezia and headed back to the boat. Our path took us right by the *Porta de Ristourante* where we could hear a big party was in progress. Peering in, Doh-Boy said, "Oh my God. Guys, look who's in there."

We quickly gathered around the window to see John on top of one of the long serving tables, apparently trying to do some sort of country dance, but it really just resembled a chicken caught in an electric fence. A crowd of locals circled around the table clapping and laughing. I scanned the room and I didn't see Cue anywhere. Which was kind of odd, because they usually hung out together at a liberty port. Where the heck was Cue?

I entered the restaurant and heard what sounded like "Yellow Rose of Texas" but, it was in Italian. As I got closer, I noticed that John's left eye was swollen, and a dark circle had formed underneath it. He didn't seem to be feeling any pain.

"Hey, Garrettt, ol' buddy! Check this out. They taught me this new dance. " He held his stomach with his right hand and put up his left hand, as though he was signaling a left turn. Then he jutted out his chin and started making the chicken-on-the-electric-fence moves again. The locals were laughing and clapping, and John looked over at me with a big goofy grin on his face. There was no indication that yesterday, he'd been dumped. Then again, maybe everything was an indication.

The people at the restaurant were evidently used to this behavior. After all; sailors come there from around the world. To exist, I guess you have to have some tolerance for someone who comes to your town and gets hammered. But, come to think of it, is it really that unusual? Can you remember a time when someone got too drunk at a party, or had one too many at a wedding and made an absolute ass of himself? I've been in the Navy for over two years and the one thing I can say is that the people in it are a slice of life. There are those that drink too much, smoke too much, talk too much, play too much and eat too much. There are those who will be your pal, your enemy, your big brother, your biggest pain-in-the-rear and those who totally ignore you. There are the know-it-alls, momma's-boys, butt-kissers, ditch-diggers and richie-riches. Just as in life. Except that, In the Navy, it's concentrated in a long black tube. People in the military are no different than civilians, except that we choose to serve our country. Maybe not that noble of a reason. Maybe it's to get a career, to get away from home, to hide out, to find ourselves, to see the world. We are here so others can sleep well, knowing there is someone on watch who is out there to protect them. Ok, how did that soapbox get in here? Back to John:

Outside the restaurant, John's face was in the shadow of an old iron street light. His right jaw muscle flexed and, through tight lips, he said," I can't believe she left me, Garrettt".

I didn't know what to say. "Maybe you just need to give her some time." Dumb, dumb, dumb. I should have stuck with more fish in the sea, or who needs her, or do you think the Braves will win the World Series this year?

He spit out, "Well, she's got plenty of that now." He looked up at the sky. "You know, she used to talk about the other guys she dated. Like she'd say, 'I once dated an anthropologist, but that got old.'" He shook his head and sighed. "Now she can say, I once dated a submariner, but blew him out of the water." He tried but he really didn't mimic her voice that well.

He was swaying and put a hand on the wall beside him to get his bearings. Insisting he could walk on his own, he listed port and starboard as he navigated down the sidewalk. By the time we got back to the boat, his arm was slung around my shoulder and I half walked, half dragged him across the brow and poured him down the hatch. All the while, he was singing "Yellow Rose of Texas". I should say he *attempted* to sing. He got stuck on "You saved my soul from hell" and sang it over and over, eliminating a word, every once in a while, like "Bingo the Dog" (There was a farmer who had a dog and Bingo was his Name-o, _ -I-N-G-O, etc.). Finally, he was down to "from hell" over and over, his eyes almost closed. I had him in his rack by then, and I thought that was it. Then he suddenly opened his eyes and threw up. Unfortunately, I was in the way. Some hit me in the chest, and the rest hit the floor. When I groaned, the COB stuck his head in through the hatch and said, "Daniels, clean up that mess." Wow, he actually knew my name now!

After cleaning up the mess (and myself), I checked in on John. He was on his back, still fully dressed and, thankfully, sound asleep. As his chest slowly rose and fell, my mind drifted back to Karen. Sure, I had a soft spot for her, but right now I hated her. That was a cowardly way to break up. She didn't have to feel or see anything that happens when you break up face to face. She didn't have to see the pain, she didn't have to endure the drive-bys, the phone calls to her work place, or the chance meetings, or give in and take him back. She knew the mail for submariners was always delayed, and she'd never have to witness the consequences of her actions. By the time John got back to port in four months, everything would be long over, with just a bittersweet memory remaining.

Tuesday, 03/31/81

Talk about the proverbial crap hitting the fan. It was 2217 hours and we'd just left the sub-tender Gilmore after only a couple of days of bliss at "the Rock". This is what we knew so far: our newly-elected Commander-in-Chief, President Ronald Reagan, had been shot. Liberty was secured early in La Maddalena. We left so fast that some of the guys didn't make it back to the launch boat from Palau, (a town in Sardinia). Side note here: Cue did finally show up, but not at La Specia. More on that later. We were steaming as fast as we could to parts unknown. At least, I couldn't say exactly where we were going. Mainly because I don't really know and, of course, no one is supposed to know where we are.

The news we got was sketchy. Some guy named Hinkley was the shooter, and President Reagan was not the only person shot. No one died, but that's about all we knew. We expected to receive a radio transmission with more details when we got close to our station in the Gulf. One concern was what the Soviets might do. Since the war with Afghanistan was over, who knew where they'd strike next if they thought our country was weak. We were prepared. There had been a LOT of activity in the Torpedo Room in the past six hours.

Since I have a few minutes, let me tell you what happened yesterday. Heck, you don't even know where we are or uh, were. When we left Pisa (without Cue) and steamed over to Santo Stefano, a rock between La Maddalena and Sardinia. Almost like being between a rock and a hard place. Sardinia is an island and tourist stop off the west coast of Italy. (I do NOT remember any of this in high-school world geography.)

John and I missed getting our clothes washed. He'd been pretty quiet and subdued since we found him in that restaurant in La Specia. I didn't mention Karen again, and he offered no more comment. So, since we had liberty and a pile of dirty clothes, we rode a skiff over to La Maddalena.

Not to see the Guardia Vecchia. Not to hit the beach. Not to hit the bars. But to wash clothes. Ah, the exciting life of a sailor! Santo Stefano is a large, touristy port. La Maddalena is smaller, more local and historic but still a tourist stop. We were directed to a laundromat in town. When we arrived, we loaded up the machines and realized we were hungry. Now, if you're in the States, finding a Hardees, McDonalds or KFC is no problem. If you're in a strange town overseas, that becomes a challenge. Fortunately, we spotted a wooden sign with hand-painted letters that boasted

"Delicious American Hamburgers". As we entered the tiny storefront, we noticed a strange medicinal smell, mixed with old wood and maybe a bit of mold, nothing really unpleasant, mind you, just not what I'd expect a hamburger joint to smell like. The windows were covered with some sort of film that made the street seem out of focus. There were two small tables pushed against the left wall and, on the other wall was a window. Not a take-order window, but one that is supposed to open to the outside. This place didn't resemble a fast-food joint back home at all. The walls were covered with old newspapers, not framed as if it signified a historic event, but more like wallpaper. A young man slid open the indoor window and greeted us. "Hola! Americano! No? Ah Si Si. Enter, enter! What would you like to eat? Eh?"

Not seeing a menu, John asked for two burgers and fries.

"Ah si si. No problem. We fix very fast. You have American money or lira?"

"Lira."

"Excellent! Now we fix. You wait. Very fast."

We sat a down at the first table which was painted a dull yellow about 80 years ago and had many marks but was clean. The two mismatched chairs were heavy, with large wooden slats in the back, they might have come from their kitchen table.

"Excuse me, sir? We don't have fries today. No potatoes. Potato chips ok? They're Lay's. Very good."

"Yes, that's fine. We also need something to drink. Do you have coke?"

"Ah good. Yes coke. 2 cokes for the fine gentlemen. We fix very fast for you."

It took a half hour. In the meantime, John went to put the clothes in the dryer. Then I went. When we both tried to leave, the young man panicked and pleaded for us not to leave. We assured him that we were just putting clothes in the dryer. His eyes were still pleading, so we told him we would go one at a time. That seemed to satisfy him. After the burgers, chips and cokes were paid for we walked back over to the laundromat to feast.

After checking the clothes, we opened up the wrappers and inspected the burgers. The spot of ketchup and mustard on the bun looked more like a mistake than something that was intended. But the burgers were thick and the buns appeared to be fresh. We looked at each other and then took our first bite. Right away, we could tell something was horribly wrong. This was not cow meat. Or if it was from a cow, she had died a long, horrible, torturous death from a disease that rotted her from the inside out. We simultaneously spit out the vile mouthful and kept spitting, trying to get every last disgusting morsel out.

"yeeeeeech". John exclaimed. That's not even close to how he said it. His face was scrunched up as if he'd eaten a lemon and he was bent over, straightening up as he started low, at first, rising in volume until he hit the "ch".

"Man. that was not beef. Or at least it wasn't cow. How many rats do you think they have on this island?" I asked.

"Well, two less than yesterday." John saw a stray dog of some mixed breed hanging around outside. This poor dog looked as though he hadn't eaten in a month. His ribs were showing and his hip bones were clearly visible. He'd look at us, then quickly look away, then cautiously look back. So, we shrugged and threw him the two burgers. That starving dog sniffed the burgers and then gobbled down the bread. Just....the....bread. He left the burgers with nary a nibble. I kid you NOT.

Wednesday, 04/01/81

Ok, I know there are no women around when we are at sea. Furthermore, I know we are sailors and we're macho (please don't sing "In The Navy" or "Macho Man" in the background). Honestly, sometimes the humor around here can get pretty gross. Case in point: On the mess decks just a while ago, watching a movie, when a blind girl came on the screen. Lipstein made a crude remark, which. I am not going to repeat here. The guy sitting next to him, a Sonarman named Kelso, chimed in. These comments were brutal and sexual. You would not hear this kind of stuff in normal conversation around normal people. Someone tried a "SHHH" but it seemed to egg them on.

What they didn't know was, that the COB had just walked down the passageway from forward of the Mess Decks and was standing there almost directly behind them. He let it go on for a couple more minutes, then leaned down and whispered something in Lipstein's ear. A small gasp jumped out of his mouth. Kelso started to say something and Lipstein's hand shot out and covered Kelso's mouth with such force that his head bounced off the bulkhead. When he tried to protest, Lipstein whispered in his ear and then Kelso went white. The rest of the movie was quiet.

I missed all this because I was on watch back aft. Much later, Cue told us in what the COB whispered in Lipstein's ear.

"Fun is fun, but those comments crossed a line." Cue said. "Some of these guys are straight out of high school. Out on their own for the first time. Like going to college. Some kids just go wild. The COB felt they needed to be reeled back in a little. So, he whispered to Lipstein that his daughter is blind."

"Wow. That's heavy." DJ shook his head.

"Yeah." Cue said with a grin. "It would be if it was true. Master Chief doesn't have any kids. He's not even married. Besides, it's April Fool's."

We all broke up then. "Mum's the word." Cue said. "Don't let Heckle and Jeckle know."

We assured him that we wouldn't.

Later, still on watch, DJ and I started talking and the subject drifted to home, as often did. "I'm going to buy some property in North Carolina," he said. His eyes had that faraway look, even though he was looking at the bulkhead. "I found some good farm land with a large pond and a creek. There's just an old farmhouse on it now, but I'm going to build a new one overlooking that pond. I'll set a two-story barn over there off the road." His hands were punctuating his dream, and his eyes flashed with excitement.

"Sounds like you've put a lot of thought into this."

"Oh yeah, but money has always been an issue." He grinned. "Not anymore. I'm going to re-up."

"Re-enlist. Wow. You sure about that?"

"Yep. Got it all worked out. Talked to the XO and the paperwork will all be ready when we pull back into Norfolk. They are even giving me extra leave to settle the land purchase."

"Wow." I repeated. "I'm a little speechless. But I guess if it's what you want to do, then here's to the future." I raised my hand for a high five which he slapped immediately with a huge smile. I haven't given two thoughts about the future and here is a guy who is making his happen. It made me a little envious. Not enough to re-up, but, still a little envious.

Saturday, 04/04/81

All is quiet as we wait for word about our President. And when I say quiet, I mean the ship has been rigged for quiet which means that, if you are not on watch, you are basically confined to your rack. No PMS (yay!), no field days (YAY!), no movie nights (Boo!) and no drills. We are somewhere in the Med. Ok, the eastern, southern part of the Med. Once a night we come up to periscope depth to receive transmissions. The sail on a sub is not like a sail on a sailboat. More like the rudder. It consists of forward planes, which resemble the wing of an airplane and, at the top, a bunch of antennas and other devices, which remind me of a Swiss Army knife when everything is deployed. We don't even need to surface out of the water. Just close enough to surface to extend whichever antenna or device we need at the time. For example, if we need to run the diesel generator, we extend the DG snorkel. The diesel needs lots of air, and we sure don't want to suck that out of the boat.

The reason we are rigged for quiet is because we're in some operational sensitive areas. Naturally we don't want to be detected. A lot of ships on the east coast were deployed when the president was shot. So, who knows how long this will last.

I read the book that Chuck loaned me. It was pretty good. When I gave it back to him, he thanked me, raised his rack and put it in an empty space he reserved for it. I have never seen anyone so neat at sea, or anywhere else for that matter. He said that he'd been on his own since his parents died. He looked up at me, then up at the overhead. His lips tightened and he blinked a few times.

"Sorry Chuck", I offered.

He shrugged, "it's not so much that as..." He stopped, looked down, then said, "Never mind". I asked him what he meant, but he said, "another time, another place." He was struggling with something, and it didn't seem like it was his parents' death. Or maybe it was. I found out the next day.

We stood watch together the next night. I say "night" but, under the water, there is no sense of whether it's day or night. The lights are always on except, of course, when there's a movie on the mess decks. Anyway, I was doing my normal roving watch and went down to Engine Room Lower Level where Chuck was standing watch. He was sitting with his clipboard in hand. The lower level is a steamy, noisy, hot, oily space. Everywhere you look there are pumps, pipes, gauges and valves painted the usual military gray. Like the upper

level, a catwalk makes its way up, over and around most of
the equipment, all the way back to shaft alley. I say "most of
the equipment" because, in some areas, you still have to duck
or twist to avoid a valve or a pipe protrusion. As mentioned
before, Chuck's a neat freak. Even in this dirty sweaty
environment, his shirt and pants are cleaned and pressed
(where does he press them?). The edges of the log sheet are
perfectly aligned parallel to the clipboard which, has one pen
clipped to it.

"Howzit goin' Chuck?"

"S'ok". Chuck grinned, although it looked more like a
friendly wince. "Starboard Condenser Pump seems a little
noisy though."

"Just run Port then." The wince turned into a real smile.
"Listen," I began, "That book you loaned me wasn't bad. Got
any other good stories?"

He left out a sigh. "Ok, Scribe." (Did I mention that was
my nickname? Can you guess why?) "This has to stay between
me and you. Promise?" I nodded. "I'm not kidding now. I'm
going to tell you some serious stuff and it can mean...", He
voice trailed off.

"Look Chuck. I can keep a secret. You don't know that
Chief Garrison was kidnapped by aliens, do you?" He looked
doubtful but threw his hands up, "All right. Here we go." I

149

was joking about the Chief. He is actually a nudist, which is something I could imagine doing because, I hate washing clothes. I mean, I grew a beard because I hate to shave. Or, you could say I'm too lazy, which I wouldn't argue with.

I knew that Chuck's parents were killed when he was a teenager and his mom's brother, Harry came to live with him. What Chuck told me that day filled me with disgust and horror. Chuck's Uncle Harry turned out to be a child molester, or more specifically, a teenager molester. What kind of monster would take advantage of a kid whose parents had died? Chuck said he was dealing with anger over his Dad's drinking that had caused the wreck and killed his Mom and Dad. He couldn't think straight, because of his parents' death and moving to a new school.

"You know, I'm not a homo," He said softly, "but I needed someone to help me deal with everything. Harry was a big help the first week. Bought me presents. Gave me money. Helped out with the funeral arrangements, and got me through all of that. Then came the day he accidently walked in on me when I was in the shower. At least, I thought it was an accident. We laughed at first and then there was a weird expression on his face. He said it looked like I worked out and asked whether I played any sports."

He stopped and looked away. By the time he got his head on straight six months later, he realized that his uncle had not only taken advantage of him, but, also a couple of other kids he knew, including an eight-year-old.

"I hated him. Not like hating school or taking out the garbage. But a hate that burned, you know, deep in me." He struggled for the right words. "Like, Like it's all I could think of. How could he do that? How could he molest those other kids? And he was getting away with it. It was so unfair." He looked me right in the eye. "I never did tell you that he committed suicide, did I?"

I shook my head no.

"They called it suicide anyway." He stood up and turned his back to me.

I was afraid to say anything. Actually, I didn't know what to say.

"While I was at school he ran a hose from the exhaust pipe of his car. I was the one who found him. I told the police he'd been depressed since the death of his sister. One cop remembered me from when my parents died. There weren't any more questions after that. I was not sorry. Not sorry at all."

Called it suicide? Was he saying he had something to do with it?

"So, I went into foster care. They moved me to another state. Stayed with a good family there." He took a deep breath and exhaled as he sat down. He looked tired. I looked at my watch and noticed that an hour had passed. We take hourly logs on various pieces of equipment, so, it made a good excuse to scoot out of here.

"That was, wow Chuck. I don't know what to say. Sorry that all happened to you. That's tough, dealing with all that. Can I get you a cup of coffee or something?"

"Naw, I'm good." He looked at me with these pleading eyes. Maybe not pleading, more like looking for acceptance, or three Hail Marys.

"Look, uh," I searched for the next word. "It's not your fault. You were a teenager and going through some difficult times."

"It was my fault."

"How? He committed suicide."

"He didn't actually kill himself." He said those words slowly and I knew what was coming next. I wanted to hear it but at the same time I didn't want. Then he leaned into me and said softly. "I kinda helped him."

I drew in a breath and slowly exhaled. The confession was so much different than Prawley's veiled comments about his mother. Right there in Engine Room Lower Level, among all the machinery and battle lanterns and noise and fluorescent lighting, Chuck spoke of what he'd been carrying inside for almost ten years. They say that more secrets are told on a submarine than anywhere else and I gotta believe that's true. Once you are away from home port and out to sea, it's like "True Confessions" under the water.

Words started tumbling out of his mouth, it's as though a pressure valve was releasing everything that was bottled up in him. His school was less than a mile from his house. He signed out of study hall, went to the library and signed in. He got a book and found a corner, laid his coat over a chair and sat down. Earlier, he had swiped a bottle of chloroform they used on frogs from Biology class. When things settled down in the library, he sneaked out and ran home.

Harry lost consciousness quickly and Chuck dragged him to the car parked in the garage. When he came home from school, it was easy to dispose of the chloroform rag. He banged out a suicide note on the typewriter about failed relationships and his sister's death. All very believable.

I admit I was torn here. I could see that the jerk deserved it. There have been times when I read something in the paper and I say to myself yeah, I can see pulling the switch with that guy strapped to the chair. I don't know whether I could kill him intentionally. Of course, I wasn't in Chuck's shoes. I didn't ask what he did with the chloroform-soaked rag or the jar itself. I don't know when becoming an accessory applies.

Chuck must have read the concern on my face because he said, "You know I'm pretty sure the statute of limitations is up but, just in case, I need you to be quiet about this. I need a friend right now, not a judge or jury."

"All right Chuck. You got it." We shook hands. We did NOT hug. We're manly men who work on a submarine after all. I wasn't worried whether or not he was a homo. I'd seen him with women at the Fifth National Banque. Although I wouldn't bet that he went home with them or that anything happened, but you can tell. I was more worried, that he would think *I* am.

"So how 'bout that coffee now?" asked Chuck. He looked more relaxed now.

"Sure, no problem. Meanwhile, I need to radio some logs."

"Yeah, me too."

With that, I headed up the ladder to the upper level. "Radioing" logs means just copying the previous hour down, accounting for any possible trends. Were we in a steady state? Did we change speeds? Any PMS evolution? That sort of stuff.

Once upstairs the legality it of it hit me. My hand shook a little as I poured a cup of coffee. Could I be an accessory? Would I go to jail? I reasoned that it was over ten years ago, and apparently, it was justified at least in Chuck's mind. Plus, it happened just that once. Later, I found out that I was wrong about that.

Sunday, 04/13/81

The President is going to be all right. The space shuttle Columbia took off on its maiden flight yesterday and landed safely. All is right with the world. We are back over at The Rock, tied up to the USS Orion and ready for some "I and I". The situation is diffused, I guess. Of course, I can't say where we were or what we did, but it was interesting.

John received another letter from Karen. At first, he was excited because he thought she'd had a change of heart. Nope, she wanted him to know that she'd boxed up his stuff from her apartment and he could pick them up at his mom's when he got back. John said he got an overseas operator off the tender and called her, but just got her answering machine. That must have sucked. His heart must have leaped when she answered only to hear "Leave a message after the beep." He didn't leave one, just hung up. It must be torture. You know, I never asked John exactly what she said in the letter. Did she break up with him because there's someone else? Or worse, someone else who is not a sailor? Hopefully this is just a bump in the road and they will get back together when we dock back at D&S Piers in Norfolk. But surely, she must have known that breaking up with him now gives him carte blanche to do whatever he wants over here.

As for Cue? He rejoined the ship the first time we hit La Maddalena. He was written up initially for missing ship's movement (Article 87 of the UCMJ) but, since he was in the hospital getting his appendix removed, it was changed to an Article 86. Evidently, he was doped up on morphine for two days, or at least that was his story. Later, he showed John and me a new tattoo with the word "Sonia" on a ribbon and three roses underneath and his appendix scar complete with stitches.

He went to Captain's Mast which is our court system. The Captain is the judge and officers are assigned as the prosecution and defense lawyers. He lost two-thirds of his pay for a month, but kept his crow. This meant that they believed most of his story, but were skeptical about some parts. Doc Baker gave him a light-duty chit for a month, but that pretty much flew out the window, excuse me I mean porthole, when the President was shot and we got on station.

Cue said he met up with Sonia the night I saw John dancing on the tables of *Porta de Ristourante* . After telling John that Sonia wanted to "get some fresh air", he and Sonia headed over to her place. Early the next morning, he was doubled over in pain and Sonia drove him to the hospital. At first, they suspected food poisoning and, by the time they had ruled everything else out and settled on his appendix, it was almost too late.

After we got back to La Madd the second time, Cue called Sonia almost every day, which was highly unusual for him. He was even sending her money to come to Sardinia since he couldn't travel yet.

The weather is warming up. Not warm enough for swimming, but that's not preventing us from going to the nude beach just west of Palau. Yeah, nude. I was a little apprehensive about going but, hey, I'm curious. So, DJ, Doh-Boy and I took the liberty launch to Palau. We hoofed it west through town to a Gilligan's-Island-looking lagoon, which the locals call "Acapulco Beach".

The first thing you see is the Mediterranean, royal blue in the deeper areas and more Windex-colored as it heads to shore. Small bushes and shrubs blanket the rolling, rocky hills on either side of a horseshoe-shaped, gravelly off-white sandy beach. Although the beach was basically empty now, much to our dismay, in the summer, this supposedly was the place for families to go skiing, windsailing or picnicking on the beach.

We kicked off our shoes and took off our jackets and shirts. After spreading out some towels we lay down on the beach in the chilly April breeze. The warming rays of the midday sun on my pale white skin made me drowsy, and it wasn't long before I was snoozing. Big mistake! DJ had found an old Coke can that he filled with cold seawater and poured it on my chest. I yelped like a scalded puppy. DJ and Doh-Boy were laughing so hard that they were having trouble catching their breath. I snarled something about payback and what that might mean. Doh-Boy was still laughing, holding his stomach on his knees, when he looked down and noticed something shiny in the sand. It was a necklace with a coin medallion of some sort, with a dude standing on one side of the coin and on the other, a Roman-looking cross which turned out to be a Saint Benedict Medal.

"How do we find the owner?" DJ asked. If we were in the States we could post a flyer or put an ad in the newspaper. My first thought, however, was, wow, what a great souvenir. It was worn, and needed cleaning, but you could tell it was old and maybe valuable. Doh-Boy put it in his jeans pocket without a clear-cut idea on how we were going to find the owner and whether it was a he or a she and whether she was old or young or if she is a fox.

After getting a tad too much sun, we headed into town for something to eat. Traditionally, dinner times here are much later than back in the U.S. of A. so we needed something to tide us over. Of course, there are no fast food restaurants in Palau, so we ducked into a place that resembled a convenience store. Maybe a small grocery store would be more accurate because they sold sandwich meat, cheeses and fresh bread, along with all sorts of unfamiliar snacks and candy. Where were the Snickers? Reese's Cups? Ruffle's? I was getting a little homesick. We settled on bread and cheese and a bottle of wine, the same snack we munched on when we saw the Leaning Tower in Pisa. We found a stone wall with some shade and enjoyed the meal. From our perch, we could see some of the city and the ocean. Such a relaxing day. I wouldn't do this back in Norfolk, buy some bread and cheese and sit on a wall. In Norfolk? But here it seemed perfectly normal. Although, come to think of it, I can't imagine the locals doing this either.

We talked about a wide range of subjects, from sports to President Reagan to food to childhood friends (Note to self: need to call Dorchester when I get back) to girls. Not necessarily in that order. We talked of John and Cue and their situations, which were almost reversed a month ago. Sometime during the discussion, DJ said, "Some friends are like footprints in the snow. They're here for a season, then they're gone."

"Ok, that sounds familiar. Where did you find that?" I asked him.

"Hallmark card." Doh inserted.

"Nowhere. It just came out."

"Sounds a little cheesy. Maybe you need to lay off the wine." Doh said.

"Or cheese." I added.

We had no way of looking it up, so we let it go, but the quote stuck in my head.

"What I mean, is there are guys in boot camp I was tight with that I never hear from anymore. I wouldn't even know how to get hold of them. Same for A School and any other duty station I've been to." DJ was on a roll. "We," gesturing to Doh, himself and me", will probably never see each other after we leave the Navy."

"Who's leaving the Navy?" Doh grinned. "I'm a lifer-dog."

"Well that's true DJ," I said, ignoring Doh's comment, "for any period of time, high school, college, whatever. I had a really good friend when I was growing up that I never see anymore. He joined the Marines before I joined the Navy and we lost touch." Sea stories are a part of life in the Navy, and it was my turn. Although it had nothing to do with the sea, it didn't matter. I had been sworn to secrecy but I figured it would be safe enough to tell them the story of Dorchester and the redhead. They probably would never meet Dorchester and I seriously doubt that they would ever meet the redhead.

Dorchester (his first name was Ephraim so he preferred Dorchester) and I met when I was twelve and new to the neighborhood. He rode by on his bike and saw me outside throwing a baseball up in the air and catching it. He circled around and jumped off his bike. He didn't even put it up on the kickstand, just let it fall. He came over, grabbed the spare glove on the ground and that's how we became friends. He was outgoing, unafraid and interested in everything, almost the opposite of me.

Fast Forward to after graduation from Marine Boot Camp, Dorchester was to be stationed at Camp Pendleton. They gave him plenty of time to get there, so he left with some guys he made friends with in boot (Wow, footprints in the snow! DJ was right!) for a cross-country trip. He didn't get into specifics but one thing he did tell me was when he met the redhead.

They had just left Vegas and pointed the 1974 Green Delta 88 west on I-15 toward LA just as the sun was easing into the horizon. They had already planned to travel along the traditional Route 66 through the desert, so they exited the interstate west of Barstow. Darkness had taken over and the guys were all swapping memories of what happened in Vegas. About this time, their headlights spotted a white convertible on the side of the road. A beautiful woman, a redhead, was apparently trying to put up the top of her convertible and was having some difficulty.

Dorchester recognized her immediately. He passed her, did a U-turn and drove up beside her car so that his car faced the opposite direction. Leaning out the window, he asked, "Having trouble Ma'am?"

She hesitated. I mean, a car full of guys, she had to be a little apprehensive. "Jello owns a ragtop. He could look at it for you." Dorchester offered. She cocked her head and said, "Jello?"

Jello hollered from the back seat, "Well Jello! How are you?"

She laughed and Dorchester grinned, "Sorry Miss Margret. He pulls that every time."

"Oh, so you know who I am. And who might you be?"

He introduced himself and the others in the car, explaining briefly the reason for the trip. She relaxed, finding out they were military and, told them her car had broken down. Since it would be awhile before help came, she was trying to put up the top. Dorchester did another U-turn and pulled up behind her so his headlights would shine on the rear of her car. Once Jello accomplished that, they leaned against the cars and waited.

"Servicemen? That is so fantastic! But how did you get the name Jello?"

Dorchester grabbed Jello's well rounded belly and said, "Because he shakes when he laughs like a bowlful of Jello." She laughed again as Jello smiled sheepishly and turned red. Miss Ann Margret said, "Aw now don't be embarrassed, Jello." And thanked him with a hug.

Far too soon, a guy in a sleek black Cadillac drove up and pulled over in front of her car. She walked over to his window and talked to him briefly, gesturing back to the car and the guys standing around her car. She came back and thanked them again for stopping and for their service to their country. She waved as she got into the Caddy and, in a moment, she was gone. It was about that time that Jello asked, "Why didn't we get a picture?"

Back in Palau now, Doh rolled his eyes and said, "Right. He met Ann Margret and didn't get a picture."

"No, that stuff happens. Why, it was just last week that I met President Reagan, the Pope and the Easter Bunny, and wouldn't you know it, I forgot my camera." DJ said with mock seriousness.

164

"That sounds like the beginning of a joke.' 'The president, Easter bunny and the pope walk into a bar and...." Doh paused.

"And what"

"I don't know what. Just saying, it sounds like a joke."

We walked around while DJ snapped some pictures. At dinner time, or at least Navy dinner time, we settled on a restaurant near the edge of town called Trattoria de Palau. The inside of the restaurant was cool and dark, still early at a little after 6 for the locals, but we didn't care. It was open and we were tired. After ordering, we worked on the next line of the joke.

"The bartender asked, "what can I get you"? I offered.

"And what?" Doh mocked.

"I don't know what. DJ?"

"So, the Easter Bunny said well I'm not real, the pope doesn't drink and the President already had a shot, so..." DJ trailed off. "Do you think it's too soon after the assassination attempt?"

"Definitely." Doh added, "Maybe we can change it from the President to a movie star or something."

"Like Ann Margret?"

"Well, maybe not her. Maybe Jerry Lewis or something."

The waiter, who spoke very good English, came over and we ordered a pizza. During our conversation with the waiter, we said that we were at Acapulco Beach that afternoon.

"Oh yes, my grandmother lost her Saint Benedictine medal last weekend." The waiter lowered his head. "She was very upset. My daughter was playing with it and lost it."

We looked at each other. Doh fished around in his pocket, pulled out his beach booty and said, "Did it look like this?"

The waiter, whose name was Ramiro, said he didn't know, but would send word to his grandmamma to see if she could identify it. Ramiro called out in Italian to a slim, middle-aged woman with long brown hair, who was busy wiping down tables. After a couple of verbal volleys accompanied with emphatic pointing and gesturing, she turned and left the room. You got the feeling that it was probably not her mother's mother who was missing the necklace.

We floated ideas back and forth about the joke and decided to leave off the Easter Bunny and replace the President with John Lennon. In the end, we added back the President. So, the punchline changed to the pope saying, "I don't drink and the President and John Lennon already had a shot". We decided against sending it to Reader's Digest.

We had just finished the main course of linguine with shrimp and maybe crab or scallop when Ramiro and his grandmother approached. She was somewhat stocky but not overweight, in a worn, printed dress. Her graying hair was pulled up in a bun, except for one strand which fell on her face. Ramiro introduced her as Mama Giordano. Doh once again dug out the necklace and handed it to her. Her eyes immediately flew wide open and her face broke into the sweetest smile. She glanced over at Ramiro, nodded and jabbered in Italian. Then she turned to Doh and flung her arms around him in a hug, as he sat surprised in his chair. Her happiness overwhelmed her, and she grabbed his head with both hands and planted a kiss on each cheek.

Of course, after we left the restaurant, we gave Doh a lot of grief about his new "girlfriend". He took it well, smiling sheepishly. Maybe too well. Anyway, from then on, we ate there whenever we could and invited John and Cue to go with us. They would sometimes meet us there later in the evening. Ramiro spoke pretty good English and didn't mind translating for us. Actually, over time, our Italian improved and we would order our favorites foods in Italian, with hand gestures and everything. But I'm getting way ahead of myself here.

Thursday, 04/16/81

We are back out to sea doing some ops. While on watch, we were standing outside of maneuvering in our normal shoot-the-breeze mode. Doh, Bernie, and Jake were there, along with Chuck and Jimmy. Victor was there too, but he is usually quiet during our conversations. We talked about Nuclear Power and how safe it is, compared to other industries. The old joke is that more people have been killed in Ted Kennedy's car than in the Nuclear Power industry. It's not abnormal to read of a coal-mine accident or someone getting killed on an oil rig. But this wasn't a debate about that. Everyone pretty much agreed that no industry has zero accidents. The conversation drifted over to cars and how they are fueled.

"You know, I heard there was a guy who invented an engine that runs on water, but the oil companies bought it so no one would ever be able to use it," Jake said.

"That's crazy." said Jimmy. "You can't run a car on water. You'd drain Lake Superior in a week."

"I heard that too, but it wasn't water, it was manure." Jake corrected.

"That's a load of crap." Doh smiled at his joke.

"The point is," Jake shot a sideways glance at Doh, "any new inventions are bought up by the oil companies, because they would put them out of business. So, it's worth it for them to seek out these inventors and buy their products."

"That sounds right, but do you have any proof?"

"No, not really." Jake admitted.

"Now, wait a minute," Doh looked at the overhead, "If that's really true, why would it stop there? I mean, every industry could do this, right?"

"Like...electric companies?"

"And toy manufacturers?" We couldn't tell whether Doh was kidding.

"Toy manufacturers?!?!?!" Jimmy laughed. "But seriously, folks, how about drug companies? There's tons of money in drugs. What if there was a cure for some disease like cancer or leukemia but the drug companies bought up the cure so they could keep on raking in the bucks?"

"That's a little morbid."

"Yeah, I have an uncle who died from cancer."

"Well, it doesn't have to be cancer." Jimmy reversed course. "It could be something else like diabetes or remember the sugar cube we took in grade school? It wiped out polio. So, the drug companies realized they'd lost all that money on

169

future treatments, government funding for research and more drugs. They learned their lesson from polio."

We were all lost in thought, trying to absorb it all. "That's scary." Doh broke the silence. "That would take a LOT of covering up, and I just don't see how they could do that."

"Oh, you mean like the Kennedy Assassination? Or that spaceship that crashed in Arizona?" Jake was flicking out a finger for each item. "Or the 'lunar landing'?" This time he questioned the quotation marks.

"Whoa now, I'm just talking about the oil industry and drug companies, not some crazy theories."

"Crazy?!?" Jake bristled. "Just because YOUR mind is closed doesn't mean you can pass judgment on everyone else. Your theory," Jake put the quotation marks with his fingers around 'theory', "is just as crazy as mine!"

We all burst out laughing, Jake's face was frozen for a second, then formed a tight grin.

"Yeah, yeah, ok." Jake looked up in the overhead. "Log time, boys." With that, he picked up his clipboard and walked away.

Saturday, 05/02/81

Time crawls when you're having no fun. We've been at
sea for a while now, doing some ops and a lot of Engineering
type drills. Every year, every nuclear boat and ship undergoes
an Operational Reactor Safeguard Exam, (ORSE) that
determines our ability to run a nuclear plant. A panel of
people board the boat with possible scenarios to spring on
unsuspecting and often unwilling participants. Basically, they
run drills on us and we respond in accordance with our
written procedures. They observe and take notes, then they
gather in the Wardroom and chortle, chuckle and guffaw at
the mistakes we made. Our actual ORSE is scheduled in the
Fall, so this is just practice. And the people who run the drills
are our own people. Today is Saturday, so we get a break,
which gives me a chance to update this journal.

We went back to the Trattoria de Palau several times
before we headed back out to sea. Each time we went, Mama
Giordano and *la famiglia* treated Doh like the prodigal son.
You would have thought he'd found the Treasure of Sierra
Madre instead of a necklace. Not that I'm complaining, I
mean, we all benefited from the extra attention. They would
bring us extra treats during the meal, whether it was a whole

steamed crab or a bowlful of steamed mussels. Then of course, a free after-dinner drink of our choice from Amaretto to Sambuca. We even sampled their homemade house liquor bottled with a stem of some tree or bush in it. Although, its name escapes me, it was pretty potent. Perhaps they made up the difference on the bill because who can figure out the exchange rate from lira to dollars without carrying a calculator around? No matter, it was still cheaper than a seafood restaurant back in Norfolk.

On our last night in port we had eight people from the boat at the restaurant. Ramiro told us not to bother ordering and simply started to bring food to the table. Soon it was filled with dishes I couldn't name. Some had red sauce with pasta and some had white sauce with pasta, plus veal and all sorts of seafood, but the one that caught my eye, was the ham and onion pizza with six over-medium eggs in the middle. They brought us wine for the meal, so we were in a great mood when the bill came. The tip we left was probably much larger than it should have been again, because it's hard to figure the conversion rate of lira to dollar in our heads, with the wine and everything. We said "cin cin", clinking our glasses as we downed the sweet Amaretto. Then, we exchanged hearty handshakes and, in some cases, hugs. We couldn't tell our hosts that this was our last night in port, but we got the feeling that somehow, they knew.

Since this was our last night in town for a while, our discussion outside the restaurant centered on what to do next. John, Cue, Jimmy and I favored the "Club de Grande", a dance club of some sorts on the outskirts of town. DJ, Doh, and two forward pukes decided to go back to the boat. We gave them some verbal abuse about their manhood and choice of sexual partners, then said goodbye once again and went our separate ways. Secretly, I was amazed that John, Cue and Jimmy would let a junior Oxygen Breathing No Load (OBNL) like me hang out with them, especially Cue. There is a hierarchy on the boat that's based on how long you've been there and, even though I qualified a couple of watch stations, I haven't got my dolphins yet.

It was a cool, clear April night in Palau as we started down the middle of the street, moving over when a beat-up miniature car approached. On both sides of us, brightly colored stucco shops and buildings stood shoulder-to-shoulder, overlooking just a sliver of a sidewalk or, in some places, none at all. The streets of Palau were a hodge-podge of paved asphalt, crushed stone and pavers. On one of the paved streets, Jimmy stepped into a pothole, twisted his ankle and went down like one of those thumb-push puppets. You know the kind I mean? You hold it between two fingers and push the button underneath with your thumb and it collapses. Release it and it straightens back up. Only Jimmy didn't jump back up. He held his ankle and rocked back and forth. "Can't they repair these streets?" he moaned.

"What department handles that?" asked John. "Do they have a street repair department?"

"Department of Transportation." offered Cue. "At least that's who does it in the States."

"Well, whoever it is," John said with a smile. "I'm sure he would look at that pothole and say, 'Hey, that's not my asphalt."

"Yeah, if he was union."

We chuckled at the pun. Jimmy was feeling better. He got up and put some weight his ankle. "It's ok," he said.

"Don't worry. If it gets to throbbin' later, Doc has some good pain meds."

"Meds in the med. Hey, that could be a song. Or maybe a book or something."

"Maybe you had too much to drink." Cue said to John. "You don't want to repeat what happened in La Specia."

'Hey, Jimmy is the one who stumbled and fell, besides I had a good reason."

"Yeah, we're not going to talk about that tonight. Tonight is about fun. Our last night in port. For a while, anyway."

It wasn't long before we came to a rather new building, with an almost-full parking lot. Well, not only full of cars. There were probably more bicycles and mopeds than cars, but it looked as though the place, was already crowded. The one-story stucco structure was set back off the road with a courtyard in front, framed with a short, stone wall. Lining the inside of the wall were assorted plants and bushes, some in large clay pots. A number of wrought-iron tables and chairs were set under a spacious green-and-white awning, which all but shielded the double doors. We zigzagged our way through the maze of tables and chairs. Large thick candles in the center of the tables provided some light, along with one window, although you couldn't see through it because of the light-colored drapes. We opened the old wooden doors, which seemed a little out of place with all the new decorations and waited in the dimly lit entrance for our eyes to adjust. We found the bar, got our drinks and grabbed a table not far from the dance floor.

The rest of the evening was mostly a blur, with a few moments of clarity. I danced with a woman with beautiful long black hair who spoke very little English. She was nice-looking but at least ten years older than me. We danced a lot and drank even more. I realized later that one of the reasons I was invited along was to buy rounds of drinks for my shipmates, which was okay with me. I wrote it off as part of the initiation, so no big deal. We don't spend money at sea anyway, unless it's poker night or someone needs a cigarette or a treasured gedunk. Gedunk is our slang for junk food, like chips or candy.

Her name was Gina, at least I think that's what she said. Like I said the rest of the evening was a blur. "She smells great!" I thought, as she sat in my lap and draped an arm around my neck. I hadn't been around a woman in quite some time, so I made a few clumsy passes which she smiled and easily deflected. I think I got a kiss on the cheek before we said our goodbyes and staggered out the door. Good thing we weren't driving. Walking was enough of a challenge. I do remember Cue watering the side of a building and then a flash of being on the liberty launch headed back over to the Rock.

When they woke me up for watch, I was dry-mouthed and red-eyed, and my wallet was a lot lighter than the day before. But I was smiling. It was nice to have some female companionship again.

.

Sunday, 05/03/81

Wow, two shocks to the system today. It started on the mess decks at lunch. I was just coming off watch and grabbed a seat next to John, who had some time off and was hanging around for the movie. Sundays are more laid back and sometimes, if you are not behind in qualification, the Chief of the Watch (COW) allows us to play a movie on Sunday afternoon. The crank brought me some food as John was telling the people at the table about the prostitute he saw the last day we were in port.

"Wait a minute", I said. "I was with you the last day in port. Where was the prostitute?" He looked at me with a smirk and said "Gina, man. I thought you knew."

"But wait a minute," I protested. "How could she be a prostitute? I didn't, you know, have any, do any stuff with her or anything. Heck, I only got a kiss on the cheek when we left."

"So, no sex?"

"Right"

"Lemme ask you. You spend any money at the Club?"

"Yeah, a bunch. The rounds I got for you guys, plus I bought a special bottle of wine for Gina."

"Which we all drank, dude. But hey, thanks." John was grinning now. "So, you spent a bunch of money on a girl and got nothing in return? And you don't think you got screwed?"

The laughter around the table (and from anyone within earshot) was instantaneous. Although I'm sure anything John said would have caused the same reaction amongst the OBNL's who were sitting there, I retorted, "Yeah, well" then tried to smile.

"Good one, non-qual." John was really enjoying this. "But seriously. You know she works at the Big Club, right?"

"When you say 'works', do you mean like a waitress?"

"Not exactly. She gets sailors and tourists to spend money on drinks and she offers companionship."

"When you say 'companionship', do uhm you mean that she..."

"That she?" John paused and made some crude hand motions indicating sex.

"Yes."

"Well, now, obviously..." He motioned with his head over at me. "Not every time." Another round of guffaws. From then on, she was known, rightly or wrongly as "Vuh-Gina" whenever the topic of Big Club arose, or Acapulco Beach or basically anything at all which could possibly be linked to it. The subject could be astronauts landing on the moon and somehow, some way, they would work in the Vuh-Gina angle. I accepted it. Of course, I had no choice, but I tried to jump in with my own Vuh-Gina references, but they fell flat and I felt a little strange afterwards. On watch, I caught myself daydreaming about a slow dance with her. I can still smell her perfume and feel the small of her back as we maneuvered around the dance floor. Her hand was smooth and soft in mine, and her body was pressed against me in all of the right places. Maybe older is better. Then something would snap me back to the present.

This time it was Chuck. I was spaced out in the lower level of the Engine Compartment when he walked up behind me and said, "Earth to Garrett."

I jumped, naturally (or actually, more like <u>un</u>naturally) which made Chuck chuckle.

"Daydreaming?"

"Yeah, well." I paused, wanting to change the subject. "How's things with you? Off anyone lately?" Looking back, I shouldn't have taken that route.

"Why, did you hear anything about happened in Palau?" Chuck eyed me closely.

I shook my head. "No, nothing. I mean nothing, about death or people dying or stuff like that, no."

179

"Relax, Garrett. I'm just messing with you." He grinned, looking relaxed and harmless as he stood there, head cocked to one side. In one hand, he held his clipboard with his logs attached and leaned against a pump with the other. "Although" his voice trailed off.

"What?" I asked, before I realized I had. The next hour was filled with descriptions of two other people (or, as he described them: "vile, evil life forms") he claimed to have "offed".

To him all VELFs (Vile evil life forms) were known child molesters. He would make contact with them, gain their trust, then figure out a way to "off" them with materials in their own house.

"Obviously, not everyone is a candidate for suicide. There would be too many questions if a preacher or politician was involved. So, I had to come up with a different way. Did you know accidents in the home are one of the leading causes of death? I don't know the actual statistic, but it's up there."

I felt as though I shouldn't be listening to this, but it was like an accident maybe a poor choice of words that, you see on the side of the road. You look to see if anyone was hurt, but you are praying you don't see any. I guess Chuck felt safe confiding in me, since no one did anything after his first confession. And, who knows, he could still be messing with me. We tend to do that on a sub…a lot.

A more recent victim was a 32-year-old VELF, who lived near Virginia Beach. Chuck had met him at a little league game in Norfolk. After a few qualifying questions, he was satisfied that he had his next target. This man owned an auto repair shop and agreed to meet Chuck behind a convenience store. From there, they went to look at some of the VELF's polaroids. Chuck proudly boasted that he always confirmed his initial qualifying questions with physical evidence. Once he'd seen the polaroids, he scanned the man's home for possible "accidents" to happen. Not seeing anything worthwhile, he wondered if a fake suicide would work. The problem with was the note. It had to be typewritten, and this guy didn't have a typewriter. Then he showed Chuck the garage. Since the VELF, did auto repair, he had a garage full of almost every automotive tool you could ask for. As an added bonus, he had a car up on a lift. Chuck marveled at his setup and the VELF was all too eager to show off his garage. When they got to the car on the lift, Chuck shied away from it for fear that the car would fall on him. The VELF showed him the how to operate the lift, lowering and raising it and, most importantly, what would make the lift drop quickly. He left the car a few feet off the ground. Chuck asked if they could crawl underneath to take a look at it. When the VELF suggested that they raise it and walk underneath, Chuck responded with that his neck was bothering him and it was easier to lie down on the crawler. So, under the car they scooted. The VELF showed Chuck all the work he'd done on this car. Chuck asked about some piece of equipment and the VELF told him to fetch a socket set and he'd show Chuck how to do it. That was the opening Chuck was looking for. He stood up, he went over to the lift and dropped the car on the VELF. That was the easy part. The hard part was making it look like an accident. He had decided on a "Rube Goldberg" kind of accident and assembled a few items. The unfortunate VELF's leg had knocked over a broom as he scooted under the car, which, in turn, hit a couple of different items (I don't remember the sequence and frankly didn't want to) until the last one seemed to trip the lift, causing it to fall. All by accident. Chuck was smiling when he said that there was an additional paragraph in the newspaper article which warned everyone to be careful when working alone in a garage.

Could it be true? Or was he simply a good story-teller? I wasn't one hundred percent convinced about everything, but if it was true, man. How creepy is it that he was in that garage setting up those things with a crushed, bloody body close by?

"Why are you telling me all this, Chuck?" I asked.

"Because it's time. I needed to tell someone. You didn't squeal when I told you what happened to my uncle." Chuck paused, his eyes pleading. "These people need to be punished, and the system right now doesn't punish them. Hell, they don't even pursue them. It's more like they stumble across these...these."

"Vile Evil Life Forms?"

"Well, I was gonna say something a lot more descriptive, but we'll go with that."

"Chuck," I carefully began, "I don't mean to say you are wrong, but the system does punish them." I reasoned this without any real proof. Then I thought, you know, Chuck has killed those people. Why am I arguing with him? I decided to stop talking, mainly because I had nothing to back up what I was saying.

Fortunately, he glossed over that and tried to drive his point home. "They don't punish them enough to fit the crime. The kids suffer for years and years over what happened to them. Do the VELFs suffer? No, they have no real remorse. They form clubs, publish newsletters and just keep on doing it, over and over again."

I agreed that it had to stop. And that I wouldn't say anything to anyone.

Thursday, 5/14/81

Getting ready for ORSE has been intense, both in training and in the drills we've been running. Since I've qualified for a few watchstations, I'm getting more involved in the drill scenarios. They are actually fun. I know I will get some groans when I say this, but it's a charge to participate in the drills. Now the training, well, that's different. The Navy brings in three or four former Engineers and/or Reactor Officers to review training records, logs and all that good stuff to make sure we are operating the reactor safely. Then they run simulation drills, which can occur at any time, on any watch, without warning.

This is my first ORSE, so I have no expectations. However, the Engineering Officer (EO), Lieutenant Commander (LCDR) Avery Samuel Soffman, is hoping to get great marks. The Engineering Officer is in charge of the men and equipment housed in the Engineering Spaces, which includes the nuclear reactor. However, LCDR Soffman gives the impression that he wants so much more. Like Captain of a Nuclear Powered Submarine or ruler of the Navy or, oh my gosh the world! Let me take you back to what he said at our first meeting about the upcoming ORSE.

"Gentlemen," he began. "we have an opportunity here, not just to do well at our jobs, not just to do well on an ORSE, but to further our own naval careers." He eyes glazed slightly as he thought about the possibilities. Then he added more about being vigilant and at the ready and blah blah blah. Not that I'm against that kind of pep talk, but it seemed insincere when he just mentioned furthering his naval career.

LCDR Avery Samuel Soffman, or "Mr. ASS", as he is called by the folks back aft is personally running all of the ORSE practice drills. (I'll shorten it to Mr. A for now).

The nice part of this is that we know when the drills are coming. We convinced the wardroom cook to watch out for him when he came in for a meal. If he had a clipboard, he would run a drill after he eats, showers and gets dressed which gives us about an hour and a half. Some people care a lot about their looks and that is fine. This guy, however, wears pressed uniforms even at sea. While all of us are in poopie suits and tennis shoes, he'd wear his normal, in port, uniform khakis, pressed and cleaned by whatever poor schmuck owes him a favor or needs a signature. So far, I've dodged that bullet.

It was close to 0700 when the wardroom cook gave us the "all clear", meaning "no clipboard", so we could relax a little. Normally, before a scheduled drill, the AEA would relieve the Throttleman so he could, uhm., relieve himself. Then he would relieve the Electric Plant Operator so he could do the same. Thank goodness for a pisser back aft which, by the way, is what we call a urinal. And when you think about it "pisser", sounds so much more civilized than "urinal". If you were just learning the English language and heard those two words you would swear that urinal was the slang. And don't get me started on which sounds worse, "fecal matter" or well, you get the picture.

So, after a round of reliefs and coffee refills for the Maneuvering watchstanders, we kicked back and talked about different ports of call. St. Croix was interesting because they could jump off the fairwater planes, which extend out on either side of the sail. Doh, who was Thottleman, had just remarked that the sail reminded him of a Swiss Army knife when the Reactor Operator noticed something wrong on the Reactor Plant Control Panel. All the rods were being driven in.

"Guys", he said calmly, "Reactor Scram."

Those two words caused a flurry of activity. Watchstanders outside of Maneuvering headed toward their

186

assigned duties while the EOOW alerted Control Room of the casualty. I say casualty because it wasn't really clear whether this was the drill or something had actually happened. About 15 seconds later, the EO, with a noticeable smirk, showed up and entered Maneuvering to observe the drill.

The boat was already at an up angle to prepare to snorkel, which means that once the sub reaches the proper depth, they'll extend the snorkel mast. The snorkel mast allows fresh air in to supply the diesel generator while the sub is still submerged. Everything went smoothly enough, and soon we were making steam again.

Once the drill was secured, the EO left Maneuvering and went forward, satisfied, no doubt, that he had surprised us. We wondered where our early warning system had broken down. Lock took out a piece of paper and, by the time the watch ended, he'd developed what he called a "Fishbone Diagram". He explained that a Fishbone Diagram helped to figure out what went wrong and how to correct it. I thought he must have had too much time on his hands. Not really knowing what it was and with no encyclopedias on board, I wrote down the phrase, hopefully to remind me to look it up at the library when we got back to Norfolk.

Since we were on watch, we didn't see what happened up forward, but we sure heard about it when our watch reliefs showed up. Since we were already at periscope depth, and the drill was secured, permission was granted to the Aux Forward to blow #2 Sanitary tank. As customary, signs were hung on the outside of all the stalls telling us not to open the ball valves for the commodes because, as mentioned earlier, the contents would be splattered all over the head at 700 pounds of pressure, instead of being blown overboard.

For some reason or another, the EO didn't get the message. I heard that the Officers' Head and the EO were plastered with, uhm, fecal matter. It took two guys two hours to get it cleaned up. Right after it happened, the EO went to the Control Room and screamed at the COW. The COB happened to be the Diving Officer and tried to calm the EO down. Mr. A, red (with smatterings of brown) in the face, demanded that the Aux Forward be written up for Dereliction of Duty, among other colorful suggestions. He raised so much ruckus that Captain Jack came out of his stateroom. He instructed the EO to get cleaned up, they would discuss this fecal matter later. The EO, I was told, looked as if he could spit nails, but left without saying another word.

After the Captain and EO exited the Control Room, things were getting back to normal when someone remarked, "Boy, he looked flushed." A round of hoots and guffaws floated around.

"And pissed off."

"More like pissed on." Another round of snickering.

"Among other things." He should have stopped at "pissed on". One joke too many. He did garner some polite chuckles.

Then the COB said, "All right men, back to work." He paused. "Now wipe those smiles off your face." He emphasized the word "wipe" and that was met with a final round of laughter.

Monday, 5/18/81

Back in port, with the sub tied up alongside the tender at the Rock, I drew duty again, while the other two sections got liberty. That's ok. Gave me a chance to relax a little and catch up on this journal once we got shore power on. Plus, we had mail call. It's always nice to hear about what's going on at home.

The amazing thing we learned was that someone had shot the Pope, which is odd since he believes in heaven. What I mean is that if you hate someone so much that you would shoot and kill him, then you just sent that person you hate to the best place ever. And *your* butt is sent to one of the worst places on earth. It just doesn't seem like they thought this through.

Speaking of mail call, Jimmy Lockridge got a letter from his wife, Shelia. They're good friends of John and Karen (when John and Karen were actually, John and Karen). Actually, Shelia and Karen were the real friends. John and Jimmy weren't really friends as much as shipmates and hung out together when their wives hung out together.

Shelia mentioned in her letter that, she suspected Karen might be pregnant, but not to say anything to John. She hadn't seen her in a month and kept dodging her requests to get together. The only reason Jimmy even told me this is that he needed to know if he should mention anything to John.

"She's not sure, right?"

"No." was Jimmy's response.

"She asked you not to say anything, right?"

"Right."

"Then don't."

Jimmy looked relieved, since he wasn't a close friend of John's. Now, I had a problem. Jimmy told me. Now I know. I *am* friends. Do I say anything? I thought about telling Cue, but his idea of finesse is a hand grenade in a hen house to get a chicken for supper. I figured, if the opportunity presented itself, I would broach the general subject of pregnancy and things of that nature. Indeed, that opportunity presented itself the very next day.

It was unseasonably warm for that time of year, so we decided to head out to Acapulco Beach. Cue sent his girlfriend, Sonia, some dinero and she met us at the launch in Palau. From there, the four of us hoofed it over to the beach. Apparently, we weren't the only people who wanted some sunshine. The beach was a lot warmer now and the thought of jumping in the water really appealed to us after the walk. Of course, since we were in Europe, some of the women were topless and I was trying not to look as we walked by, wishing I had some dark sunglasses like John. He turned and grinned at me after we passed a couple of nice natives, as though he knew what I was thinking.

We found a nice spot toward the west end of the sandy beach and dropped our stuff. Cue and Sonia had the foresight to bring a blanket to lie on. We had just our beach towels, which were our only means of drying off. As Cue and Sonia started to spread out their blanket, we kicked off our tennis shoes, shed our shirts and scampered down to the water's edge. After toe-testing the water, we dove in. Cue joined us with a huge splash, and we spent the next few minutes engaging in general splashing and doing handstands and the usual things you do when you haven't been in the water since last year.

And oh, the water! It was fantastic! It felt as if weeks of grime and grit were being washed away in the crystal-clear blue salty waters of the Mediterranean. Acapulco Beach is in a cove, which opens up to the Mediterranean Sea. It's not unusual to see yachts, cargo ships and power boats dragging skiers and wind surfers in this area. After a week of seeing only the interior of a sub decked out in Sea-Foam-Green, Battleship-Gray paint, it was nice to be able to look farther than twenty

192

feet for a change. And it didn't hurt that the scenery was awesome. John and I decided to grab our snorkel masks, so we navigated our way over to our pile of stuff next to the blanket where Sonia now lay topless. Yep, I said topless. Talk about your awesome scenery.

I wished right here I could say I was "cool, calm, and collected" about that whole situation. About her lying there topless, eyes shut, with no tan lines shimmering with a fresh coat of suntan oil.

"Do you want fries with that?" Cue asked without humor. He'd walked up behind me, dripping wet, and caught me staring a tad too long. Sonia's eyes popped open and, unlike Cue, she was looking at me humorously.

"Uh, no, I'm good." I stammered. "I just came-"

"You just came?" Cue asked.

"No, I mean. I was looking-"

"You were looking?" Cue asked again.

"Uh, yes. I mean no. Not that. At that. Or them. There." Pointing at Sonia's 'theres' was not helping. "I was looking for my snorkel mask."

"And you thought perhaps it might have been on Sonia's chest? Now why would you think that?"

John decided to join in the fun. "Yeah, Scribe. Why would you think that?"

Sonia leaned over, her breasts rolling gloriously to one side (I think my head may have rolled a little to one side, too), and grabbed a bottle of suntan oil.

She then looked up at me innocently and teased with a smile, "Maybe it's time for me to get some sun on my back. Could you please rub a little oil on me?"

I smiled nervously and my right hand acted on its own and moved outward. Then my brain kicked in and screamed STOP! I quickly glanced at Cue, who looked as if he would break off my hands and beat me with them. My hand snapped back like a rubber band and I lowered my eyes, mumbling, "Oh no. Sorry. Heh, heh. That's Cue's job."

John and Sonia chuckled at that and Cue finally relaxed. John and I grabbed our snorkel masks and proceeded to get our backs sun burnt as we floated and snorkeled, fascinated with the world beneath the clear blue waters of the Med.

After a time, I became more comfortable with Sonia's lack of clothing. She even joined us in a little Frisbee tossing. Of course, being a rookie, she had no clue how to throw the thing or even how to hold it. Cue showed her the basic grip, and soon she could flip it fairly well. Although, occasionally, the errant flip would land near a couple or a group or, if we were fortunate, in the water. It's always more fun to dive for the Frisbee and hit water instead of sand. We moved further down the beach to a more open patch of sand. This made allowances for Sonia's errant tosses and gave us more dives out in the water.

One of Sonia's errant tosses landed near a slightly overweight, nude, very white man, sunning himself, belly up with a wet towel on his face. The Frisbee kicked up some sand on him, and he jerked the towel off his face to protest. At that moment, I realized I was seeing a whole lot more of Chief Garrison than I wanted to. Quite the contrast between Sonia's display case to Chief Garrison's.

And yet again, I found myself staring at places that I really shouldn't be staring at. I guess it was just the oddity, the abnormality, of seeing Chief Garrison's sausage and eggs on full display against the beautiful backdrop of the Mediterranean. It's like when walking into a room and spotting the red-wine stain on a white Persian rug. Or being at a high-school football game and spotting a pimple on a cheerleader's face. Your eyes are just naturally drawn to it.

"DANIELS!!" The Chief's yell brought me back to the present.

"Sorry about that, Chief." Yeah, I went with "Get Smart".

"It's about time to flip those eggs, ain't it, Chief?" I said over my shoulder, while moving quickly away.

After a spectacular meal, back at Trattoria De Palau, John and I said our good byes to Cue and Sonia. As they headed toward Sonia's motel, we made our way back over to the Club de Grande. This was a night for drinking. No social interaction was needed or wanted or desired. We found a table away from the action and ordered our drinks. We sat in silence for a time, drinking in the atmosphere and the semi-warm beer. When John spoke, his question seemed like an intrusion, somehow.

"Did I ever tell you how we met?" John was watching a couple on the dance floor with a slight smile on his face.

"Karen, I mean. Did I ever tell you how we met?" He had turned his head to me and the expression in his eyes was like sweet sadness. Like when you were a kid and saying goodbye to grandma. No that's not it. Like when you take your daughter to the store, get out of the car and suddenly you realize she won't reach for your hand anymore. That's not quite it either but it's close.

"No, don't think so." I said, shaking my head slowly because shaking it too fast was not a good idea. "Let's hear it."

"We're playing a softball game against the USS Sea Devil. They were getting ready for a WestPac and we just come back from running Ops down at Andros Island. It was a beautiful Saturday in July, not too hot, not too cold. We loaded the gear in the duty van and drove across the road from the D&S Piers to the park." John lit a cigarette and took a drag, savoring the memory.

"Well, just outside the gate was a grungy band of hippies protesting the war or nuclear power or bras or something. Anyway, as we drove past them, I noticed Karen standing next to a red-headed dude with a megaphone. He was shouting some nonsense, but as we passed, and I know it sounds corny and all, but as we drove past them, our eyes locked for a moment. Well, not a moment really, but it was more like two heartbeats."

"Who, you and the red-headed dude?"

John gave me an annoyed look, rubbed his chin and continued. "SOOOO when we got over there, I'd realized I forgotten my shades and borrowed the van to go back over to get them. I grabbed the sunglasses out of my car and drove back. As I passed the group again, I stopped and mouthed the word 'Hi'. She mouthed back 'Hi'. I motioned for her to come over and, to my surprise, she did. I told her about the softball game and invited her over when she was finished with all that protesting. The red-headed dude was getting annoyed and shouted at her. She said she had to go, mouthed 'bye' and turned around and walked away."

I ordered two more semi-warm beers as John caught his breath. "So, I guess she showed up?"

He nodded. "Yeah. Yeah, she did. Even though she looked out of place in her hippie clothes, she clapped and cheered us on, right along with the other wives. That's where she met Jimmy's wife. Man, she got the lowdown on me before I even knew her full name."

"And she still went out with you?"

Another annoyed look, but he continued. "We made a date for the next weekend. I suggested the beach but she smiled, tilted her head to the side and asked "Why? So, you can see the goods?"

As he was reminiscing, I was trying to decide whether if I should tell him that Karen might be pregnant. If she's not, then no good will come of this. She might just be cold and aloof, which would send John into a tailspin again. If she is pregnant and the baby is not John's, that would also send him into a tailspin. If she is and the baby is his that would send John into a…well…tailspin. No good could come from telling him, but I couldn't help it.

"Have you thought about calling her?" I tried to ease slowly into this like you'd ease into a hot bath.

"Sure, I thought about it. But the time difference and the availability of the tender phone made it difficult. And I wasn't sure what her schedule was…" His voice trailed off. "Besides, if I called and she wasn't home, her answering machine would have picked up. How do you talk to one of those things, anyway? 'Hi, this is John. How are you?' It sounds so like grade school." He shook his head at the thought. "Actually, what I did" he took a breath, then exhaled, "was…I wrote her a letter."

Whoa. This was new information. He'd never even mentioned that he wrote her. This might be the perfect way to break the ice about this. "Man, you never told me that. What did she say?"

"She never wrote back," he said slowly and took another sip of beer. "So, I wrote again. No response. Not a peep. I thought about asking Jimmy to ask his wife if she's even still in Norfolk. You know, whether she is seeing anyone or gained hundred pounds. Maybe she is having second thoughts. Maybe she thought she made a huge mistake. But," he paused again. "I don't think I want to know the answer."

"Well, not a hundred pounds." It slipped out before I even knew I'd opened my mouth.

John blinked twice, turned and stared at me. "What do you mean, not a hundred pounds?" He scowled. "What have you heard, Garrett?"

This was at the point when you realize you can't get the torpedo back in the tube. "Well, just that some people have wondered if you know that maybe it's possible, you know, that she might be pregnant."

John leaned toward me which was a little intimidating. "And **who** exactly are these people?"

I told him what Jimmy had told me. It all came tumbling out in what felt like one super-long sentence. When I finished, I took a deep breath and exhaled a sigh of relief. John sat there and took it all in. Then he said, "Ok, I need to call her."

"You know there's no proof whatsoever. We don't really know. We were just guessing." I offered.

"Yeah, but now I need to find out."

"What are you going to say? Hey hi, how are you? Everything is fine here. Oh, by the way, I saw some cute pregnancy clothes in Palau today. Can I pick up anything for you?"

"I have no clue what I'm going to say. I'll think of something."

That ended the night. Well, not ended. It actually just began a different chapter. We left the club and headed back to the tender. We didn't talk much. Once John blurted out, "Wow, I could be a daddy." "Or not", I reminded him. He scowled at me again. I second guessed myself about telling him a million times. We were on the launch leaving Palau and he was drumming his fingers impatiently on the bench seat. His plan was to get an overseas phone or ship-to-shore or some way to call Karen before we pulled out again. When we tied up to the pier at the Rock, he pushed his way thru the drunken sailors and ran up the brow of the Orion.

I let him go. I couldn't watch.

Tuesday, 5/19/81

John tried to get in touch with Karen on the tender that night but couldn't. The closest he got was an answering machine, and, obviously, he couldn't leave a message. How can you leave a message like that on an answering machine? Considering the time difference, Karen was probably still at work. If she could still work, that is. Or maybe she was at her doctor's office to learn the sex of her baby (or even *babies*). Maybe she was finalizing her wedding plans with the real father or is walking down the aisle right now. Maybe she decided to have an abortion and is going under the knife right now. Maybe she left Norfolk altogether and went to West Palm Beach to see her mom and raise the baby down there.

I have to get these ideas out of my system right now so I don't accidently spring them on John. If the guys on the boat knew anything about this, they'd be ruthless of course, at first. But in the end, they would be very supportive. Well, at least some of them would.

We are underway again. The plan is to do some submarine maneuvers that I can't really talk about, and then steam to a more suitable area for some Engineering drills in preparation for our upcoming ORSE. I've been busy studying for my watchstation, qualifications plus getting sigs to get my Dolphins, which could easily take a year.

Cue has become the epitome of a love-struck sailor. This is a huge switch in his "a different woman in every port" philosophy he preached so fervently.

The Engineering Officer or "Mr. A" has recovered from his surface-spray coating courtesy of Sanitary #2 and is trying to whip us poor slobs into shape so he can garner a good score for the ORSE.

By the way, Bernie does a great impression of the EO. We were back on watch again, at our usual hang-out just outside Maneuvering. Bernie had just finished the following rendition, complete with facial expressions and hand gestures that cracked us up. It went something like this:

"Ok men. We have a daunting task in front of us. Daunting! As you know, ORSE will soon be upon us. It is my sworn duty to whip you poor slobs into shape, so we will run every drill I can find to make you feel like the complete waste of human flesh that you are! What's important here is MEEEEEE (he motioned back at himself with his thumbs). Don't forget that, men! The ORSE is to help MEEEEE (again with the thumbs)! Because a good score on the ORSE might get me a promotion. An excellent, oh my god, an excellent…Well, that would get me promoted off this floating sewer pipe, away from you peons who can't tie your own shoes. Maybe on to a cushy job in NAS or, dare I even think it? Yes, I MUST! Washington, D.C.!?!?!?"

As much as we complained about them, drills were actually a good thing. They kept us on our toes and prepared us for a possible emergency. It also broke up the monotony. I honestly don't mind them. Of course, there's not that much to do for an Auxiliary Electrician Aft. Phone Talker is usually my primary responsibility. The good thing about that is you hear how the drill is going, and who's screwing things up. Usually you are the first to know when the drill is secured.

However, drills are only part of the score for ORSE. Record-keeping and cleanliness are also elements, back aft anyway. Everything has to be cleaned, stored, inspected and then cleaned again. So, our Friday field days have increased to four hours. Sure, we clean at first, and some clean the whole four hours but our group? After the first couple of hours, mostly we try to find places to hide out. It was during one of these field days that we got the idea to use Bernie's impersonation skills (Could he be the next Rich Little?). We just didn't know how yet.

Back in my rack and I couldn't sleep. I dug out the newspaper I bought before we got underway, hoping to do the crossword puzzle. What caught my eye instead was a headline "Auto Repair Shop Owner Death Suspicious". I read the story and went to find Chuck. He was on the mess decks, settled in for the movie. I whispered in his ear and asked him to follow me downstairs. We ended up in Aux Machinery 1 and I showed him the article. Amazingly, he was stone faced.

"Thanks Scribe. I had a feeling something was wrong about it. The article explained that the death looked staged and was turned over to homicide. A security camera caught the dead guy and a mystery man at the gas station. Police were questioning people and had a couple of leads.

" Don't worry Scribe." It sounded more like he was reassuring himself. "They don't have nothing yet."

He went back upstairs to watch the movie and I went back to my rack, no longer interested in crossword puzzles.

Wednesday, 5/20/81

Another day, another casualty drill. Or two. Each watchstation back aft needs to have drill scenarios run because we have no idea when the ORSE board will run the drills or what kind of drills. That means multiple drills, sometimes in the morning and sometimes in the afternoon. Curiously, never in the evening, though. I asked why and John just shrugged and grinned, "Officers need their beauty sleep, Scribe." I hadn't thought of that before. For some of the brass, a day at sea is no different than a day in port. Except that they don't go home, of course. They maintain the same schedule while underway: breakfast at 0600, lunch at 1200, and dinner at 1800. We slowly run through the time zones travelling east, so there is no real jet lag. We pop up in La Specia at 0800 and it's morning to some of the officers. Meantime, some of us just got off watch and want to hit the rack before embarking on some other adventure. Well, that's not entirely true. Some will jump off the boat as soon as it ports and rest later. A lot of forward pukes have no immediate duties and can leave as soon as the brow is across.

There is a ton of stuff the nukes have to do to bring on shore power and secure an engine room.

The forward pukes were doing a lot of grumbling about participating in these ORSE drills. Almost all of them affect the forward watch stations in some way or another. Sometimes we even have to go to snorkel depth and run the diesel generator. Besides getting the A-gangers involved, this affects everyone sleeping in the Bow Compartment, because the diesel makes that space hot and noisy.

To be fair, Engineering (the nukes) has to support the regular Ship's Drills that the Forward Pukes run periodically. And they are so very important, like "Low Coffee Level in the Goat Locker" and "Loss of Cherry Pie in the Ward Room". Ok maybe those are not the ACTUAL drills they run. But that's not saying that you want to be anywhere near the Goat Locker when there's no coffee.

After the drills, the off-going watch station has to muster in the Torpedo Room to go over the drills that were run. The EO talks in a low voice, and everyone has to crowd around him to hear, because it's a strain if you are in the back row. Not every person back aft keeps to a regular bathing schedule. So, who you stand next to makes a HUGE difference.

We usually get there before the EO, so the off going EOOW makes sure everyone is there. If there are any stragglers, he sends someone to fetch them. The EOOW is normally, but not always, a junior officer, usually an Ensign, eager to make a good impression and move up that chain of command. They follow commands and procedures to the letter, and that can make them easy targets for a prank, which we love to pull at sea.

We were all gathered after watch in the Torpedo Room after one such drill. The Torpedoman on watch tolerates these things with a roll of his eyes, then, usually grabs his logs and walks around the Torpedo Room to get away from them. This time however, the Torpedoman was Cue, and he was sitting at the Fire Control Panel with the rest of us when the growler went off. Cue answered the 2JV, listened and said, "Hold on, Sir."

He handed the 2JV to the EOOW, Ensign Hawthorne, who, no doubt, took great pride in getting us all assembled and on time for the drill debriefing. Ensign Hawthorne took the 2JV and, because he is tall and the cord was short, he had to bend down to put his ear to it. We heard him say, "Yes Sir." Then, "Ok, Sir." And then, "Right away Sir." Ensign Hawthorne straightened up, then handed the phone back to the Torpedoman, and said, "Hang this up for me, PETTY Officer." It was almost as though he emphasized the word "Petty" on purpose. Cue mocked him with a "Hanging up the 2JV, SIR", rolled his eyes, grabbed his logs and left.

Ensign Hawthorne commanded, "Ok men. We need to get to Aux Machinery 1 on the double. The EO is there waiting for us."

We looked at each other, and someone mouthed 'On the double?" We all shuffled dutifully out of the Torpedo Room and into Aux Machinery 1, just aft of the Torpedo Room. I haven't been in there that many times, no nuke has really, for that matter, or anyone else on board except for A-Gangers, which made it an odd choice to muster there. I was not sure what was in there but I can tell you that the space itself was small. We barely fit, and we could tell pretty quickly that the EO wasn't there.

"Maybe he went up to the Galley." DJ offered.

"Or he was abducted by aliens."

"Or listening to REO Speedwagon in his stateroom." We snickered at this because the EO does it a lot. Not that REO Speedwagon is a bad group. It's just that the EO is much older than we are and you'd would think he would listen to groups more around his age. Like CCR. Or The Beatles. Or Guy Lombardo.

Ensign Hawthorne held up both hands and, yes, kinda yelled in a strained voice, "Focus, people." He looked around the room and pointed at me. "You. Go to the Torpedo Room and see if the EO is there. You." He stabbed his finger at someone else. "Go to the Mess Decks and see if he is there. You." Another victim was selected. "You go to the EO's Stateroom and see if he has left. The rest of us will wait here until we get a report."

Because I left first, I didn't hear all the other assignments. As I opened the Torpedo Room door, I could see the EO was sitting on the bench at the Fire Control Station. Emotionless, he motioned for me to come up to him.

When I got close, he said in his typical, low voice, "Where is everyone, Petty Officer Daniels?"

"Waiting in Aux Machinery One, Sir." I replied dutifully.

What I didn't know was that Aux Machinery One got growled after I left. The voice imitating the EO commanded Ensign Hawthorne to go to Maneuvering, because Ensign Hawthorne, I have to review logs and write the Night Orders after the drill debriefing, and Ensign Hawthorne can you make it snappy?

A little frantically, the Ensign again shouted a little too loud, "Ok, everyone to Maneuvering, and make it snappy!!" Someone mouthed the word 'snappy?'. The Ensign sent DJ after me and hurried everyone up the stairwell to the mess decks. He directed someone to get the man he sent to the EO's stateroom and hurried the rest of the pack up the stairwell by the mess decks, through the hatch back to the Engineering spaces.

"So why are they in Aux Machinery One, Petty Officer Daniels?" the EO asked still emotionless. He was writing some notes in a log book, presumably the notes from the drill scenario.

"Ensign Hawthorne got a message from you, and said we had to go to Aux Machinery 1 "on the double"."

"A message?" He put down his Montblanc pen and fixed those cold gray eyes on me. "Explain 'message'."

I scratched the back of my head. "Well, he got a call on the 2JV…"

"He who?"

"Uh…who? Oh, Cue."

"Who is Cue." It must have sounded like a Doctor Seuss book. It was clear that the EO was getting impatient.

"The Torpedo Watch." I finally managed to say. At that moment, the aft Torpedo room door flung open and DJ yelled at me "Let's go, Scribe! We're meeting the EO back at ma..neu..ver…ing." He dragged out the last word, syllable by syllable, as he realized that next to me was the EO, sitting like a girl on the bench seat. I said that because his legs were crossed with one knee over the other. I think, as you get older, the way you cross your legs, among other things, changes. The normal way to cross your legs is with your ankle on the opposite knee. But, at some point in life, maybe after you get married, you begin cross your leg over your knee.

Anyway, we told the EO what had happened and why his Ensign beat feet back to Maneuvering.

The EO's eyes (did they really turn red?) showed more emotion than I'd ever seen. He jumped up and stormed out. DJ and I looked at each other and shrugged. Now what?

The Mystery Growler had apparently upped the stakes. Not satisfied with just growling random stations, he added impersonations. Now, though growling random stations are a nuisance, the Mystery Growler has crossed the line by technically impersonating an officer (UCMJ, Article 134), according to the EO.

What we didn't know and would soon find out, the EO marched straight to Captain Jack's Stateroom and complained (whined?) about what happened. The EO indignantly said someone had impersonated him and demanded action. But how can you find a ghost? How do you determine who does impersonations? Do you put everyone on trial? Of course, we had our suspicions about who it was, but none of us was going to rat him out.

So, what did they do about it? Obviously, the guilty person who did this was not involved in the drill. So, Captain Jack gave the EO permission to interrogate under the UCMJ every nuke who wasn't on watch.

Now, big picture, you would think that the ORSE would be more important than spending a lot of time on this witch hunt. After the next watch, the EO met with the whole watch in the Torpedo Room, and outlined his plan. He encouraged the guilty party to step forward. Someone asked how anyone could be sure that it was a nuke. The EO replied with an icy stare that they knew that the growling had come from back aft, which we all knew was a bluff. Then, one by one, he called everyone who wasn't involved in the drill back to his stateroom and grilled them. Since I wasn't part of the interrogation, I asked Jimmy what had happened during his time with the EO. The EO indicated someone had already given up the name and he just needed someone to confirm it. Then Jimmy smiled at me and said, "I told him I don't even remember what I ate at midrats."

The interviews were repeated after watch for the next few days. There was so little time off after watch anyway, and now the interviews, as they were called, were cutting into our sleep time, movie time and shower time. The EO was hoping someone would crack. Of course, we figured out the culprit was Bernie, but no one let it slip out about his impersonations. The EO asked the Captain to start interviewing the non-nukes and we believe that's when the Captain put the kibosh on the investigation or at least we think he did.

John asked me later if I knew who had done it. I told him I honestly didn't know for sure, but he had that skeptical look on his face. "You mean, like you didn't know about Karen?" he half-jokingly asked.

"John, you know that was different." I said, defending my actions.

John shrugged, smiled and said, "I know Scribe. Water under the sub."

"But if I had to make a guess, I'd say it was Bernie." I offered, feeling a little like a rat for betraying Bernie.

"Yeah, that's what I'm hearing from the forward pukes," John said. We were down in Aux Machinery 1, away from the rest of the crew. It was a safe place to be. Nukes didn't venture down there much. The A-Gangers were the only forward pukes who did. Thank goodness, the HPAC wasn't running, or we wouldn't be able to speak without yelling.

214

"I hear they're planning to secure liberty for the nukes at our next port of call, unless someone fesses up." John was digging out some dirt from under his nail with his pocket knife as he spoke and then looked over at me.

My Spidey sense went off. "Did someone tell you that?" I asked. "Or did someone tell you to tell me that?" It's no secret that John and I are friends. It's a little unusual for pukes and nukes to socialize, much less to strike up a friendship. He looked up at a valve in the overhead.

"Look," he began, as he glanced at the door, "I was asked to ask you that by my LDO, who, I can only guess, is buds with your LDO. But this," he moved with his finger back and forth between us, "does not go beyond that door." He finished using that finger to point at the door.

"John, honestly I don't know KNOW." I emphasized the last word. "Bernie is really good at those impersonations of Mr. A. I think Mr. A suspects him and just wants to punish us to make him to confess. As for me, I'll take whatever punishment it happens to be. Probably most of the guys back aft would say the same thing. We're not going to rat, and I really don't want anyone to own up to it. The witch hunt Mr. A has put us through surely caught Captain Jack's attention and he probably put a halt to it. I don't think he would allow Mr. A to actually secure our liberty at a port over this. And even if Mr. A did secure our liberty, you can bet that we'd screw up his ORSE." It was well known what this ORSE meant to Mr. A.

"Well that's something I can pass along to my LDO, right?" said John.

I nodded. "Just leave my name out of it." I said. His LDO would know anyway.

"I'll tell him I heard it over the 2JV." He grinned. "Let's go see what the movie is tonight."

"I gotta hit the rack. We have more drills scheduled tomorrow."

He groaned. "Just tell them not to do a reactor scram. I don't want to have to snorkel tomorrow."

"As if I have control of that. Have you heard what's the next port of call?"

"Sousse, Tunisia."

"Is that even a real place or are you just making it up?"

"Oh, it exists, alright. 'Port of Call – Sousse, Tunisia. Where men are men and camels are nervous."

"They have camels there? Can you ride them?"

"Sure, for a price. Just don't let one spit on you."

Thursday 5/28/ 1981-Sunday 5/31/1981

Well, he did it. In an obviously desperate move, the EO, Mr. A, pulled the trigger and secured our liberty for Sousse, Tunisia. I am not even sure where it is or what is there, but I sure ain't gonna see it now. The Nukes are pissed. It hasn't even been proven that a nuke did it, but Old Flabby Sides (one of his new nicknames, the others were not so nice.) did it anyway.

The news has dominated our discussions outside of Maneuvering. Some think it's just a bluff; that he'll back down once we pull into port. Others don't believe Captain Jack will permit it. There have been many, sideways glances at Bernie, who looks too guilty. Now, when he walks up, no matter where we are; the mess decks, back aft, or in the berthing spaces, everyone clams up. Bernie says 'hey, guys. What's up.' The others just mutter 'hey' or 'hi, Bernie'. We'd all agreed not to implicate him, but then we treat him like a pariah. Do we think he should confess? Well, Bernie posed that question to me in Engine Room Upper Level. I was Aux Electrician and he was standing an Upper Level Watch. We were between the Main Engines, out of earshot of the

EOOW, talking about the Braves when suddenly he looked over at me.

"So, Scribe, do you think I ought to confess?"

"Confess what?" I asked innocently.

He rolled his eyes. "I get out next year. In April. I don't want to screw that up." He scrunched up his face. "But I really hate seeing Mr. A win this. What he's doing isn't right. It's vindictive."

"I know. He's been way over the top about this. I can't remember when we had our last drill."

"Well, we pull into port on Monday, and I don't want to screw up liberty sooooo, I'm headed up to the EO's stateroom after watch to confess."

"Are you wanting me to talk you out of it? Because that would be pretty tough." I said with a grin.

"Nah. I'm good. I'm hoping Mr. A will drop everything once he knows who did it. I will act all scared and everything, you know. Promise not to do it again. That sort of thing."

"Well, I hope it works out for you, Bernie."

"Don't tell the others, ok?"

I said I wouldn't. Dutifully after watch, Bernie, hands stuffed in his pockets and head down, walked slowly forward to the EO's door. He met Chuck in the passageway just forward of the mess decks. Chuck gave Bernie a wink, and told him not to worry about liberty now. Surprised, Bernie asked why. Chuck said he just confessed to being the Mystery Growler. Chuck slapped Bernie on the back and left him standing there in the passageway with his mouth open.

Later, when I asked Chuck why he would do that, he said he had his reasons.

Mr. A worked quickly after that. Some said he had paperwork already filled out and was just waiting for a confession. The charges against Chuck were for violating Article 134 of the Uniform Code of Military Justice (USMJ) plus Article 88, Contempt toward Officials; Article 89 Disrespect to an Officer; and Article 107, False Official Statements; all of which could send Chuck to Captain's Mast. In my mind, I saw Mr. A cackling with glee as he typed it up in his stateroom. Not being up to speed on Captain's Mast, I listened to the scuttlebutt going on outside of Maneuvering and on the Mess Decks. And there were lots of opinions about what would happen.

"He doesn't have to agree to it," said Jake. "He should have a lawyer with him if he does." As usual, we were outside Maneuvering, and Jake was hanging out with us. Bored, I guess. Or just wanting to talk about the Captain's Mast. Jimmy was at his usual spot as Electric Plant Operator and Mr. Galloway was the EOOW. Victor had the Reactor Plant, and DJ was on the Throttles. I, of course, was standing my usual Aux Electrician-Aft watch.

Victor rolled his eyes. "Where are you getting a lawyer while we're underway?"

"Well, not a lawyer per se, but if it goes to Mast, they'd assign him an officer to help with his side of the story." Jimmy said in a matter of fact manner. Jimmy, the senior Electrical person, gave the impression he knew what he was talking about.

DJ looked troubled and was quiet up until now. He placed his coffee cup in the black toilet seat cup holder (well, that's what it looks like) and said, "How do they even know that he was the Mystery Growler?"

"Uhm…he confessed?" Jake said mockingly.

"He didn't confess to being the Mystery Growler, did he? I thought he just confessed to imitating Mr. A."

Mr. Galloway cleared his throat and corrected, "That's Mr. Soffman." We turned, open-mouthed, toward the EOOW, kinda shocked he would number one, correct us, and number two, use that…'officer' tone.

"Well ok. MR. Soffman." Jake mocked.

DJ looked frustrated but it was not clear why. Victor, sitting ramrod straight, looked a little bored.

Then Mr. Galloway floored us.

"By the way, I have been assigned to represent Chuck during his Captain's Mast. You may want to hold off any more discussions or revelations about the case, unless, of course, someone here wants to confess to clear him." He said the last part with a smile. "That would make my job a lot easier."

"You think he's innocent?" Jake asked.

"Not for me to decide." Mr. Galloway deflected. "Besides, he already confessed. The question is, is there evidence somewhere that could somehow point to his innocence? Was he on watch? Did someone see him in his rack while this was going on?"

Behind the EOOW, the back curtain to Maneuvering was open. Bernie had just walked up from behind Maneuvering, clipboard in hand, as though he'd been he was taking logs the whole time. He sauntered up between the Turbine Generators, but glanced over me before he returned to his logs. You could tell he was trying to nonchalantly listen to the conversation.

Chuck was taken off the watchbill, pending the investigation and Captain's Mast. It was scheduled for Saturday, just two days away but that's a long time if you just went port & starboard watch in Engine Room Lower Level. Those guys were not happy.

Little did Mr. Galloway know, but Little Willie, the Yeoman, kept us updated about the case. Since the Yeoman's office was adjacent to the XO's stateroom, he could listen, using a glass jar pressed against the wall. The trick was getting the glass jar in just the right spot so you're not listening to the back of the XO's closet. Little Willie showed me the area which was directly opposite of the XO's rack. The rack acted like a large earphone which perfectly transmitted any sound in the XO's stateroom. "There are some sounds you can't unhear though," confessed Little Willie. "Those will live with me." I wasn't sure what he was talking about and really didn't want to open that bottom drawer.

According to Little Willie, Captain Jack was against any punishment. There were several discussions involving the XO and the EO and the XO and the Captain. As near as we could tell the Captain and the EO didn't discuss anything about the case, just normal operating issues. We were more concerned about what punishment would be handed down. According to Little Willie, the keeper of the books on this stuff, since there was no intent to defraud, the maximum punishment would be a bad-conduct discharge, forfeiture of all pay and allowances, and confinement for 6 months.

Finally, Saturday arrived and the Captain's Mast was slated for 1300 hours in the Ward Room. That's 1:00 pm in civilian time. I was on watch back aft. We had guys stationed on the Mess Decks outside of the Ward Room, ready to relay any news back aft to those of us on watch in the Engineering Spaces. Mr. Hawthorne was relieved as EOOW at noon, so he could give his version of what had happened.

It took less than a half an hour. The verdict was 'not guilty' of impersonating an officer but guilty of lying, Article 107. From Little Willie's account, Mr. Soffman, who acted as his own council, stood up and pompously listed the charges. He called Mr. Hawthorne as his witness. Captain Jack, his head resting on one hand had a slight smile on his face as Mr. Hawthorne recounted the wild goose chase he was sent on. Captain Jack then pointed at Mr. Galloway and asked if there was anything the defense would like to add. Mr. Galloway asked Chuck to do his impersonation of Mr. Soffman. Chuck tried, but just couldn't pull it off. Mr. A said, 'how clever' and that all he needed to pretend that he couldn't do impersonations. Mr. Galloway then introduced a witness who had seen Chuck in the shower during the ruse. Captain Jack looked at the EO and said sternly, "Avery, I gave you a lot of latitude in this. But we have an ORSE coming up this year and we can't be fooling around with this crap." Captain Jack

223

dropped the charges down to Article 107, lying to an officer. Liberty was secured for Chuck at Sousse, and he had to spend the days in port cleaning back aft with no reduction in pay or rate.

After everyone filed out, Mr. A protested the verdict. Captain Jack lit into him again, "Have you run any more drills since this happened? You asked to pursue this, which I granted, with the knowledge we would still be in preparing for ORSE. Your thirst for revenge has overridden your duty to my boat." Mr. A again tried to say something, but Captain Jack cut him off. "If you don't zip it right now, I will write YOU up for dereliction of duty, not preparing Engineering for ORSE and guess what? You will be busted and booted out of this man's Navy, because the last time I checked, I am still the captain of this boat."

Of course, the good news for us back aft was that liberty was unsecured. Desecured? I don't know the nautical term but we're going ashore tomorrow at Sousse, Tunisia.

DJ was a bit unnerved about the whole thing and had second thoughts about re-enlisting. "I talked to the XO, and he said to sleep on it and not to make any rash decisions. So, I did. In fact, I slept on it several nights. I just told the XO to hold up on everything. Apparently, they'd been working on a new deal. To sweeten the pot, they said they would guarantee that my shore-duty assignment would be taking care of the shore power connections in Europe."

"You mean like what Gail did?" She was in charge of our Shore power connections in La Specia.

"Yep, apparently her rotation is up. She's headed stateside. The XO rattled off places like Holy Lock, Scotland. Roda, Spain…a bunch more I can't remember."

"Well, good for you, right?"

A little more subdued, he shrugged and said, "Well, it's just for two years, then back to a boat for two years. Then I've got the rest of my life on the farm." He turned his eyes toward the bulkhead, like he could see 2000 miles away. "Yeah, it'll be good," he said flatly, trying to convince himself, hoping I would either talk him out of it or talk him into it. I was non-committal.

"Well, good luck DJ, whatever you decide." He thanked me and we went our separate ways, he to his future and me to my rack.

Monday 6/1/ 1981

I remember a Bugs Bunny cartoon when Bugs was in an Arabian desert and a sheik or someone was chasing him with a giant sword saying, "Hassan chop." It's funny how these things can influence your expectations, when you actually visit someplace like Sousse, Tunisia.

A quick survey topside and dockside didn't reveal any tents or desert or women dressed in belly-dancing clothes. And where were the camels? For those with neither maps nor rate of Navigator, Tunisia is located northeast-ish, on the continent of Africa. Sousse is a coastal city tucked in the Gulf of Hammett, a port town much like La Specia. Stacks of cargo and ocean-going vessels dominated the north side of the docks, while the pleasure and commercial ships populated the south and middle. In the city, buildings that are various shades of brown and white rise just past the coastal road which was filled with cars, trucks, and mopeds but again…no camels!

The night before we pulled into port, we were given our usual briefing on local customs, exchange rates and places to avoid. A bank would arrive on board to exchange our American dollars with the "funny money", or what we called anyone else's currency in the world. One of the tidbits of information was not to pick up any food with our left hand. Apparently, that's the hand they wipe their butts with, and it's considered unclean, since toilet paper isn't always available.

Another fact that stuck out in my mind is that the number-one religion is Muslim, which I know nothing about, except Muhammed Ali and Kareem Abdul Jabbar converted to it. The Muslim religion has very strict rules. Women must dress in a certain way and you could go to prison for three years for Homosexuality.

Kelso cracked, "So, we can't hold hands on the beach?"

The COB responded dryly, "Kelso, you and Lipstein are ENCOURAGED to hold hands on the beach."

Laughter erupted and shouts of "zinger" and "COB got you" and other coarser phrases were bandied about.

Other cool facts that I recall: co-ed Turkish bath houses are popular (that got Cue's attention); Bobby Fischer withdrew from a chess match there; we should stay away from the mosques unless invited; camels spit; haggling is expected when selling in the marketplace. The Bank representative came down to the mess decks and exchanged our US dollars for their "funny money". I wondered if the Captain knew this guy (he seems to know everyone at every port) or this was a regular thing they did.

With Captain's Mast behind us and ORSE in front of us, this was our chance to forget about the sub life for a while. White sand beaches that went on for miles combined with the blue waters of the Mediterranean make a popular European tourist spot. But before we hit the beach, we wanted to check out the local cuisine and buy some touristy souvenirs. Leather goods were dirt cheap, and the same goes for jewelry. Being guys, we didn't know much about rings and such but, we stocked up on leather goods. Once we got our feet on dry land, we headed over to their city mall, or medina. John said he'd meet us at the Medina, then disappeared, looking for a phone or something to reach Karen. He had received a familygram from her two nights ago. Although he didn't let me read it, ("It's coded, Scribe. Even if you read it, you wouldn't understand it.") apparently it meant that they were back together again, which was a huge relief to me.

Sousse, Tunisia. Now this was more like it. The city seemed monochromatic, with buildings largely tan or varying degrees of off-white. Like Italy, the cars were small and old-looking. Traffic was punctuated with pedestrians, mopeds, and donkey-drawn carts.

The Medina in Sousse resembled a stone-walled fort, complete with what looked like gun-turret towers. Once inside, you could browse the shops in their indoor "mall" or head out to the courtyard in the middle. The shops were not in rooms so much, but lined along the wide hallways. As you passed, the merchants were not shy about shouting "Ah, Americans" and pointed out the quality and inexpensive prices of their specialties. What kind of specialties? There was a wide assortment of rugs, scarves, pottery, purses, handbags, tote bags, belts, rings, bracelets and necklaces. We were told that the leather was genuine but I couldn't tell from which animal. Anyway, it was cheap, so I scarfed up a leather tote bag for 30 Dinars, which I hope is a good deal. I am never too sure whether the dollar is worth more or less than a dinar, but I guess I'll figure it out when we cash back in. Some shops let you pay in American dollars, too. John caught up with us, and we split off from the other guys and took a seat on a stone bench. He showed me some silver necklaces he bought Karen, and some multi-colored scarves.

"I can't buy her any clothes because I don't know what would fit!" he chuckled.

"I'm just glad y'all are back together. What changed her mind?"

"I told her I wanted her and I wanted the baby. She was a little surprised I knew about the baby." He glanced at me. "But she was scared. Her parents don't know, and they're some rich couple down in West Palm Beach. I told her not to worry. We'd go down together when I got back into Norfolk and break the news. There was a lot of crying and then I told her I loved her, which meant more crying."

"You or her?" I interrupted.

"Yeah, I might have gotten a little misty there, too." He said with a grin. "I don't even know if I realized it myself until recently. I was lying in my rack one night when it just hit me. I loved her. I wanted to be with her. Only her.

When she broke up with me. I ain't gonna lie. That hurt. These past few months have been rough, so rough. It didn't matter whether she had seen anyone else while I was gone. I mean, we weren't exclusive. We didn't say the "L" word or anything. It was just great to be with her, you know. They say that absence makes the heart grow fonder. Well, it did. I missed her. So, I decided, after I got back to Norfolk, I wanted her to pick me. And she did. Before I even got back. Life is good, Scribe."

After we had our fill of shopping, which didn't take long, John got one of the strikers to take all our stuff back to the boat while we ventured out to the beach. This was no small cove like Acapulco Beach. This beach was gorgeous (can I say gorgeous and still be a man?), white sand stretching out as far as the eye could see. No nudity here that I could see, not that

I was looking for it (ahem). We were told we were safer on the beaches near the motels and, since we looked like tourists from the motels, we wouldn't be questioned.

We ventured into the pool area of a large chain hotel west of town, which was directly across the street from the beach and hung out there for a while. Some of the women were sunbathing European style, while the guys slyly tried to snap some pictures. However, Bernie wasn't shy at all. His camera was a top-of-the-line SLR camera that he wore hanging from his neck on a thick colorful lanyard. He would walk right up to the topless women with his fancy camera with some line about free-lancing with fashion magazines which I suppose could have been true. It almost always worked, which amazed me. Could have been the way he dressed, I suppose. He didn't look touristy or like he'd just stepped off a Navy sub. He'd set up his tripod in front of flowers or statues, and women would simply walk up to him. He told me he liked taking pictures of everything; really, he does. Maybe I'm too critical of his motives.

Once when we were on watch, I asked him what kind of camera he had. He tilted his head a little to one side and asked, "Do you know what an F lens is?" I didn't so he went on to explain what it is and why he would choose one camera for some activities and a different one for others, how filters

231

work and reflective screens and a litany of other things I can't even remember. "But," I asked, when he finally paused to take a breath. "What kind of camera is that?"

"Oh." He was really getting into cameras and all so he was a little disappointed to stop. "It's a Nikon."

"Oh okay. Like that Simon & Garfunkel song. Uhm....'I own a Nikon camera. I like to take the photographs'."

"Yeah, like that song." He nodded and, maybe it was me, but it seemed a little condescending. "What kind of camera do you have, Scribe?"

Now I felt a little embarrassed by my obvious camera deficiency. "It's a Kodak Instamatic." The look on his face was kinda like when you are trying not to yawn in someone's face and don't want them to know. Except, in this case, I think he was trying not to laugh. I went on, "It's great, you know. When you take the last picture, you can drop the whole thing in the mail or at a store with a drop box."

A chuckle slipped out and he said, a little too enthusiastically, "Well that certainly is handy!"

After watch, on the mess decks, he walked in with photograph albums in hand. Now, I am not big on seeing other peoples' vacation or baby photos. So, I was a little apprehensive. Bernie's biggest passion was wildlife photography, but not the kind of wild life photos sailors

232

normally see. He pulled out an album with amazing shots of bears, eagles, deer and other animals. He said that sometimes he had to wait for hours in blinds just to get the shot he wanted. I asked him if any of those animals were in his freezer and his face showed a flash of annoyance before he chuckled and said, 'No, just old enemies'.

I gotta say, the pictures were impressive. Looking back over my time there on that boat with those guys, it would have been nice to be able to take high quality shots that reflected more of my memory of those events.

So, Bernie, being Bernie, got into a conversation with two, exotic-looking, dark-skinned ladies by the pool. They wore colorful one-piece bathing suits cut high up on the hip with plunging necklines. The women looked to be in their twenties. They said they were from Cairo and had just finished their first year of college. I have a difficult time speaking to women of my own race, so his ease in talking with them astounded me.

I nudged John, "Check out Bernie over there." I tilted my head to the left and he glanced over.

"Lucky him." Then he smiled, "I had a black girlfriend once."

"Really?"

"Oh sure. Women are women, no matter what color, age or shape they come in. They all want to feel special and loved and for you to be faithful to them."

"So, what happened?"

He hung his head and sighed. "I wasn't faithful. My mistake. Hey, I'm getting hungry. Let's see if this hotel has food in it."

We left Bernie and the others and headed to the lobby of the hotel. Sure enough, they had food there so we tried their chicken kabobs and couscous which was new to me. It resembled rice but tasted nothing like it. Served in a bowl, the broth was rich and spicy and the veggies made it look like a thick stew. All in all, it was like taking a bite of the Mediterranean.

While our outing was uneventful, COB had what could be considered an international event. It wasn't until after we had left Sousse and got underway, that I heard the whole story. I actually gave up some rack time to hear it because John said the COB got radical in Sousse. We were in the bowels of the torpedo room as Cue, in hushed tones, filled us in.

"This," his head swiveled from side to side, "This is a no-shitter. I got this from the COB himself." Note: true sea stories are commonly called no-shitters.

234

He sat back on the bench seat and grabbed a sip of his Navy coffee. "Do you remember those two girls from Cairo that Bernie met? Well, guess who ended up with them later that evening."

I shrugged. "Who?"

"Lipstein and Kelso." He paused again to let that sink in.

John and I looked at each other. "No way." John blurted out.

They were the last two people on the boat that anyone would have guessed would end up with these two gorgeous girls. Or any girls for that matter.

"Yep." Cue nodded with a smile. "Those two hot girls actually WANTED to hang out with Lipstein and Kelso."

"How is that even possible?" I wondered.

"Well you know these guys. They tell huge stories, always bragging about what they can do, who they know and how much money they have. Once, they even went so far as to tell Doh that their grandparents were the Rockefellers." He leaned back again. "It was that particular lie that got them in trouble.

Those morons told those young ladies the same thing, you know, their grandparents are the Rockerfellers and how rich they are. Those idiots had all their money converted to dinars and were flashing it around like crazy. Completely fooled those girls. They bought it hook, line and sinker. The boys asked them to dinner and the girls said yes, and excused themselves to change out of their bathing suits. So off they went to change and those idiots were high-fiving each other.

What those wizards of smart didn't know was that those two, innocent young ladies not only changed but told their boyfriends about meeting some rich relatives of the Rockefellers."

"Wait. Their boyfriends?" I was confused.

"Yep." Cue nodded. "Their boyfriends. Those ladies were not from Cairo or even in college. They were there with their boyfriends to rob rich young white kids on holiday. Victimless crime, right?"

"Except the robbing part."

Anyway," he continued, "their plan was to get our boys drunk, which quite frankly wouldn't have taken much, then roll them in an alley somewhere. And it almost worked. When they went out for drinks, the girls drank watered down drinks. Meanwhile, our boys were doing shots to impress them, at their urging, I'm sure.

It wasn't long before Lipstein and Kelso, totally wasted, were walking down the street, arm in arm with two gorgeous ladies who, let me tell you, were dressed to kill."

"Literally," inserted John.

Cue nodded. "Just by chance, the COB and Chief Roberts were leaving the restaurant and couldn't believe their eyes when they looked out the window. There goes Lipstein and Kelso, arm-in-arm, with two hot women and not far behind them, were two men. Obviously thinking something was wrong with this picture, the COB and Roberts decided to follow them from a distance. It wasn't long when one of the girls motioned to an alley, and they all went in." He paused again, relishing the moment.

"The COB and Roberts rounded the corner just in time to catch Lipstein and Kelso getting the crap beat out of them, with the girls yelling encouragement to their boyfriends. Cob yelled for them to stop and one of the them turned around and said, 'Who's gonna stop us, grandpa?'

COB and Roberts looked at each other and COB said, with a smile, 'we are'. Well, Roberts was a black belt and the COB was a former boxing champion well, in Norfolk anyway. It wasn't long before they had those two punks on the ground and who shows up but the police, or whatever they call then in Tunisia."

"Constables?" John asked.

"Bobbies?" I added.

"The fuzz?"

"Coppers?"

"Stop it you two. Besides, bobbies are in England. So anyway, the girls told the cops they were jumped by the COB and Roberts. The cops took them all down to the station, and Captain Jack was summoned. Well, you know that he knows everyone in about every port we pull into. He made a couple of requests, an official was notified and 'viola'! Our guys were released back to the boat and the punks were arrested. It just so happened, this wasn't the first time they tried this."

"How does he do that? Know people in every port?" I asked.

"Well, he's been around, plus I'm sure the Navy makes their own arrangements. I heard about a little old lady who owns a pier down in St. Croix. Every time a Navy ship or sub pulled in, she showed up with her beer wagon, and the crew was instructed to buy a beer from her, whether they drank beer or not.

Besides, I heard that Captain Jack had a special closet on board, full of gifts that he passes out when needed."

June 23, 1981

Among all the drills, training, and plotting dots in the Med, we got an unexpected port visit in Athens. Greece. We had to anchor in the harbor, which meant that the Nukes had to steam again. I had duty on the first day but the second day, John, DJ, Doh and I took the liberty launch to shore, eager to taste the local flavors. Food, too. Who am I kidding here. Just the food.

First impression? Athens is like any other large metropolitan city in the States. Traffic, sidewalks, lights, tall buildings and people dressed in normal clothing. A far cry from Sousse. I expected togas, Roman columns, and sandals. A little disappointing.

We got on a tour bus which took us to the Parthenon, located on a hill overlooking the city. Even that was kinda anticlimactic. It looked like an unfinished construction project. Don't get me wrong, it was cool to see, but it kinda made you look around and say, "Nice. What's next?".

Once back in the city, we got a cab and asked the driver to take us to an authentic Greek restaurant. He dropped us off in front of a seaside restaurant, located east of the city near a marina. The host lead us out to a table located right on the beach, with gorgeous sunset view of the Mediterranean.

Wine, prawns (their word for shrimp), fava and moussaka, we were sharing our dishes and drinking a fabulous house wine. A photographer noticed us and asked to take a picture "of the happy couples."

DJ and Doh started to protest but John took a different approach. He grabbed my hand and said, "Thanks! This is our third anniversary together!"

I picked up on it, "Yes two years of bliss and one year of (sniff) heartache."

"Now, honey. You're not going to bring that up again, are you? We're celebrating."

"You're right, as always, dearest."

Doh and DJ were dumbfounded. After leaving a modest tip, the photographer gave us a polaroid, bowed and approached a couple seated near us. Worried, DJ leaned over to me and asked, "Don't they jail homosexuals here?"

John dismissed him with a wink and said, "That the Sousse way. Not the Greek way!"

As darkness began to fall, we could see the lights on a ferris wheel slowly spinning to the east of us. Squeals, faint laughter, and calliope music drifted over to us, so we made our way to a seaside carnival set up in a parking lot by the marina. It seemed familiar, but in a dream-like kind of way. Sure, they had food there, but where were the elephant ears?

Sausage with peppers and onions? Replaced with gyros (pronounced "heroes") and baklava-looking stuff. Suddenly I felt very homesick, longing to be around familiar surroundings.

We walked by a table that had a small washtub contraption with a colorful sign that declared "Spin Art!". John was immediately drawn to it, saying the design looked like tied-dyed t-shirts. He asked if I thought Karen would like it. I shrugged and nodded sure. I really just wanted to get back to my rack, close the curtains and shut out the world. Instead, we waited for John to choose his colors he thought Karen would like. It took him three tries before he was satisfied. DJ and Doh drifted off, talking to group of young women. I watched as they separated two of them from the pack, local ladies who would have a story to tell their children one day. Doh looked over his shoulder and waved, then gave me a "thumbs up". I smiled and waved back, and they disappeared into colorful crowd of people. John had just finished his spin art. While it was drying, I asked him if he wanted to head back to the boat. The liberty launches went all the way up to midnight, but we were pulling out tomorrow afternoon.

"Sure Scribe. Had enough?"

I nodded glumly.

"This place getting to you?"

Again, I nodded, as I looked off in the distance.

"This is your first Med Run, isn't it?"

"My first *anything* run. My first trip outside of the US."

"You know, there's a name for that. Culture shock. Look, everything's temporary, man. Soon we'll be back in port, eating McDonald hamburgers, and you'll catch yourself thinking about eating baklava in Greece. Athens, *Greece*. Not grease…grease."

"Grease is the time, is the place, is the motion." I sang.

"Grease is the way we are feeling." John joined in. Keep in mind that neither one of us can sing so we were pretty much off key.

We stopped there because people around us were giving us odd looks.

"Our third anniversary!" John shouted. The crowd nodded and sauntered off. "We'll always have Greece, sweetheart."

The Humphrey Bogart impersonation was cheesy, but I felt better. Still homesick but not drastically so. The spin-art was dry, so we maneuvered through the throng all the way to the end of the carnival. DJ and Doh were perfect gentlemen with the two local ladies who, in turn, were perfect ladies.

Although Doh embellished the scar on his arm with a shark attack while saving someone's puppy while in the Med.

I left Greece, tired of new places. Tired of strange places. Tired of submarines. Wishing for something normal. I made a vow that when we got back, I would take off to some beach...no, enough ocean...some lake somewhere in the mountains with real trees, and sit in the sun.

Epilog August 1981

I say 'August', only because that was when we pulled back
in to our port, docked at Pier 21 at D&S Piers. I thought
Channel Fever was bad before we pulled into La Spezia but,
let me tell you, it was nothing like it was after we surfaced to
steam our way into Chesapeake Bay. People were antsy,
milling around the mess decks, as if they'd been drinking that
Goat Locker Coffee. People walked back aft who were not
even on watch, hanging around Maneuvering. Loud
conversations were usually punctuated by laughter and high
fives as the discussions shifted to who, what, when, and
where, they were going to do to who, what when and where,
when they got their feet back on dry land.

I wondered how everyone's cars, trucks and bikes would
operate after sitting in the parking lot for five long months.
To be honest, I wondered whether my 1974 Nova was going
to crank, or even if it was still there Well it was, and it did
crank. But some unfamiliar songs were coming from that
country station I listened to. But, I'm getting ahead of myself

After the boat docked, the lines were secured and the brow was set, I poked my head up topside at Pier 21 for the first time since winter and breathed in that steamy, salty Norfolk air. My eyes drank in the familiar sites, smells, sounds of my country. Wow, signs were all in English! A military band was playing music, and a small crowd of family and friends were gathered to greet us at the front of Pier 21.

John was finally reunited with Karen. Yep, she was actually there, waiting on the pier with Rick's wife when the tug pushed us into our slot. Last night, John shaved, showered and even ironed his uniform (seriously, where is that iron?). Often, we stretch out our uniform under the mattress to get the wrinkles out, but there were actual creases in his pants and shirt!

He was topside of course, craning his neck to get a glimpse of Karen as the topside crew was storing the lines.

I was back aft, waiting with DJ to get the shore power cables down the escape trunk. Again, I poked my head up thru the escape hatch and scanned the crowd. There was no mistaking her. Six months pregnant in a bright yellow sundress, maternity of course. Later, John told me that it was similar to the dress she was wearing the day they met many months ago. Only, similar because it would never fit her now.

And she had done something different with her hair. It was longer and curlier than I remembered.

The crush I once had on Karen was over. Maybe it was the fact that she was preggers, or maybe, I just realized that she was, is and always will be, John's Girl. Nah, I think it was that pregnant thing.

John spotted her and shouted her pet name. She smiled sweetly, waved and looked down. We wrestled with the shore power cables and got shore power on in record time.

Finally, I wandered across the brow and maneuvered my way through the happy crowd to catch up to John and Karen. They were off to one side, John with his foot on the bumper of someone's car, talking to Rick and his wife, his arms waving at whatever story he was telling. Karen was standing next to Rick's wife and their kids. Rick's little girl stood next to Karen, her little curly head leaning against Karen's hip. Karen's motherly arm was around her shoulder. John wrapped his arm around Karen's waist, and her hand slid into his back pocket. It was nice to see them together again. It gave me a sense of peace, though I don't know why.

When I walked up to them, Karen broke free long enough to give me an awkward hug. I say "awkward" because I didn't want to squish her belly, so I leaned over and hugged her shoulders.

After polite greetings, I said, "So, have y'all set a date?"

They looked at each other, mouths open then looked off to opposite sides. I immediately regretted asking it.

John looked down at the ground, kicked a loose rock and said, "Well, it's complicated. We need to uh, I mean. *I* need to meet the family first. I may not have the right blood type." He grinned and looked at Karen. Karen slapped his arm. "Stop it! They'll love you." She said without conviction.

"So, are y'all headed up there, or are they coming down here?" I have got to remember to think before I speak! "Or do they even know?" Someone STOP me!!

"Well, they know." Karen began haltingly. "They know about John. But they don't KNOW about John. They don't know his…uhm…profession."

"Yeah what a shocker for Mumsie and Daddy." John joked.

"It will be ok. I just want them to meet John before they know about him."

John spoke up, "Hey Garrettt, you should come with us to meet her parents. You can talk me up, you know, like a job referral or something. And hey!" John pointed at Karen, "Karen's twin, Callie, will be there. So, you know." John winked at me.

Evidently, I don't have much of a poker face, because they both laughed.

"Well...cool...hey, twins...does she look like...I mean does she have the same..." I stumbled.

"She's Identical, physically, if that's what you mean," said Karen. "But we have VERY different personalities."

"Well then, I'll come...I mean, I'll be there." Again, the brain was having trouble processing all this information. "Not that your personality is bad or anything else is bad...or good." They laughed again at my awkwardness, so I shoved my hands in my pockets and said, "ok, well, I've got duty tonight, so I'm gonna take both feet out of my mouth and use them to walk back to the boat."

John nodded and said, "See you tomorrow, Scribe."

I got halfway down the brow and looked back at them. They were caught up in themselves, smiling, talking, touching. It made me ache a little that I was missing that connection, that emotion in my life. Perhaps when I meet Callie. Who knows? It was a lonely walk back to the sub. As I headed down the hatch, the familiar aroma of diesel fumes and sweaty tennis shoes drifted up, welcoming me back for one last night before my two days of freedom. That night as I lay in my rack, my thoughts drifted back to John and Karen. I sifted through my memory for anyone who was as special to me as Karen was to John. Maybe Candace. Maybe it's time to give Candace a call, or send her money to come visit. Visiting her would probably be out of the question.

Or does that seem too needy or desperate? All these sailors who left the boat today went back to their wives or girlfriends (or in some cases, both…ba-da-bum bum). And kids! Normal lives with normal wives. Maybe it's time for me, too. Ah well, too much thinking, and I can't do anything about it now, anyway. After my last supper on the sub for two days, I crawled into my rack and pulled out a book, hoping to read until I got sleepy.

But I just couldn't focus on the words in the book. I read the same paragraph at least three times. I wasn't even sure I was on the right page. Being back at home port left me with mixed emotions bubbling up inside, like a lava lamp.

It kept coming back to me that tonight, all over Norfolk, families were sitting down to supper, reuniting after a five-month absence. Laughter would punctuate the animated stories told around the table. Accomplishments and milestones would be highlighted. A daughter's baby teeth, a son's baseball trophy, a wife's dealings with the DMV. And, of course, there would be sad things to share. An aunt's death, a teenager's broken heart, the passing of a family pet. Catching up on over five months of being apart, unable to share day-to-day happenings, frustrations and joys. It had to be a rough time for those maintaining the home fires.

Weeks have passed, since we pulled back in to home port at Pier 21. The summer heat is gone, replaced with cooler temperatures, and the air has a certain crispness. There's talk of a Northern Run coming up soon. We're getting the boat in shipshape condition, and the tender is handling the major items. Some special equipment to use up in the Northern Sea has been loaded and stowed. I've only heard rumors about what it's used for.

Some loose ends to tie up here. It was just a couple of weeks after we pulled in, that Cue brought Sonia over from Italy. We gathered at the Fifth National Banque a few times and she fit right in with everyone. Knowing more than one language is an advantage. It multiplies your chances of meeting someone. I made a mental note to learn Spanish the next long deployment we make.

Chuck disappeared as soon as we docked. In hindsight, the transformation of Chuck's appearance the last two months of our deployment was totally logical. He grew a beard and gained some weight. Bernie, on the other hand, lost weight and shaved his beard. Like me, Bernie had the first duty day when we pulled in. Chuck left as soon as the brow was across, dressed in Bernie's uniform all the way down to military IDs. The reason they switched was just in case the cops were looking for Chuck when we pulled in.

Sure enough, Chuck's luck appears to be running out. A detective did want to question Chuck about the "accident" the auto repair shop manager had. He was on the pier when we pulled in and talked to the Duty Officer after everyone who was off duty disembarked. Only Chuck wasn't there, of course. Bernie told me later he'd agreed to switch places with Chuck, who actually had that first duty when we pulled in. Bernie, having more seniority, was off.

So, this was the tradeoff that Chuck had arranged with Bernie for taking the fall for him during Captain's Mast. Chuck suspected that the cops would be sniffing around, and he was right. They questioned several of us about Chuck, his background, relatives, where he lived, that sort of thing. I told them that Chuck had been molested by an uncle, but that's all I volunteered. After all, did I really know that Chuck had done what he said he did? I had no real proof. It's widely known that sailors can bend the truth a little for a good sea story. Heck, that's what makes them sea stories. Cue's description of the way COB took down those hoodlums could have been an exact recount of what happened, or it could have been embellished a bit. Who cares in the end? It made a good sea story.

251

I got a letter from Chuck not long after he disappeared. It came in a plain white envelope with no return address but it was postmarked Coral Springs, Florida. I destroyed it after I read it, because he asked me to, so I can't reproduce it here. The gist of it described his search for the killer of a kid in Florida. He felt he was getting close, but the search took him to an underbelly of wickedness he never could have imagined. He spoke of a close-knit society which preyed on these kids, and exposed him to things he wished he'd had never seen. He said he sent plain brown envelopes full of incriminating information to the Broward County Sheriff's Department. According to him, there have already been some arrests. He said he was through with the whole vigilante thing. For his sake, I hoped he was. I think of him now and then, when I see an arrest made of a child molester. I hope he is still out there somewhere. The Navy listed him Unauthorized Absence (UA) and to my knowledge, they haven't found him.

Now for some good news. A date has been set for John and Karen's wedding, Jimmy's wife will help her with the wedding plans, since we have an upcoming Northern Run and we won't have as much outside contact as the Med Run. John said there are venues to consider and Karen's parents, since they are footing the bill, so he is going along with it all.

"After all, the honeymoon is the important part, right?" John winked at me, but his eyes looked a little too wide-eyed.

Speaking of wide-eyed, once we got back into port, DJ left for North Carolina to attend a re-enlistment party in his honor. While there, he planned to look at some farm land. Good thing he didn't buy any.

The summer of 1981 saw an increase in drug tests for the Navy. While we were in the Med, fourteen sailors aboard the USS Nimitz were killed and many more injured in an aircraft accident. Seven planes were destroyed and a bunch were damaged at a cost of over $150 million. Six of the fourteen who were killed had marijuana in their system.

When he got back to the boat, DJ was routinely drug tested, and he failed. He told me later that he'd had just one joint the night before he drove back to Norfolk. He and some friends were down by the lake fishing. It seemed harmless. He figured it would work its way out of his system before he had to do a piss test. "I can't even remember the last time I had a piss test." He shook his head and ran his fingers through his hair. "So now, busted in rank and shipped out to an aircraft carrier."

"Which one?"

"Enterprise."

"Say hello to Captain Kirk for me." I was trying to lighten the mood. DJ smiled and shook his head again. He still was upbeat about the whole thing. Maybe it was his Christian faith. Maybe it was his nature to let things roll off his back like water off a duck.

"I still have to honor my two-year extension. They didn't remove that. But guess what?" He turned to face me again. "I still get to do the shore duty overseas. That's not a nuke billet."

"Are you going to see Gail?"

"We'll see. Nothing's definite yet. We have to look at schedules and stuff. I won't even start that duty until December."

"Hey, we'll be on a Northern run then. Maybe we'll see you over there."

"Hope so." We shook hands and DJ walked off to a whole different life than he planned a month ago. Heck, after five months away from the US, a lot of us are headed to a different life. The Pope and President Reagan were shot. Prince Charles got married to a school teacher, I think. A spaceship took off and landed back on earth for the first time. A cable channel now plays nothing but music videos. I kid you not.

Until next time, RA-SEP, y'all.

KEEL LAID: 26 July 1965
LAUNCHED: 16 December 1966
SEA TRIALS: 8 October 1967
COMMISSIONED: 14 December 1967
LENGTH: 292 Feet
MAXIMUM DEPTH: In excess of 400 feet
MAXIMUM SPEED: In excess of 20 knots
DISPLACEMENT: 4,060 Tons
SHIP'S COMPLEMENT: 106 Officers and Men
NUMBER OF TORPEDO TUBES: 4

INACTIVATION
CEREMONY

Following 24 years of proud service

17 August 1991

**Norfolk Naval Base
Norfolk, Virginia**

255

USS Lapon Sail located at

American Legion Post 639

2660 S. Scenic Ave.

Springfield, Mo.

417-882-8639

Crews Mess looking starboard aft

Crews Mess looking starboard forward

Looking Aft Starboard

Looking Forward Port

Starboard Sail Planes

USS Lapon Underway

Med Run 1981

Acapulco Beach, Palau

The Rock

Liberty Launch Boat!

Medina at Sousse, Tunisia

Keith Post (center) welcomes some of many visitors to
St. Marys Submarine Museum.

Contact information for "Bubbleheads"

Facebook: Steven Brock Author

Email: steventbrock@yahoo.com

Website: bubbleheadsthebook.com

CPSIA information can be obtained
at www.ICGtesting.com
Printed in the USA
BVHW042241040720
582980BV00016B/696